YOUR TAXES & SAVINGS 1991-92

AGE Concern

BARCLAYS

Published by Age Concern England
1268 London Road
London SW16 4ER

©1991 Age Concern England
Thirteenth Edition

Editor   Lee Bennett
Design   Eugenie Dodd
Production   Joyce O'Shaughnessy
Copy Preparation   Marion Peat
Printed and bound in Great Britain
by Grosvenor Press, Portsmouth

British Library Cataloguing in Publication Data
Your Taxes and Savings 1991-92 — Revised
I.Taxation and investment advice for older people
II. West, Sally; Hawthorne, Jennie
III. Age Concern England 336.240942

ISBN 0–86242–106–3

Age Concern England would like to acknowledge the
generous financial sponsorship provided by
Barclays Bank PLC to allow this book to reach a
wider audience.

The publishers would also like to thank Katherine Cowlard
of Age Concern England and John Kennett and James Tew
of Capel-Cure Myers for their invaluable help in checking
factual information in this book.

CONTENTS

Other Financial Options   *99*

Further Information   *113*

FOREWORD

Barclays Bank's relationship with Age Concern spans many years, so we were particularly pleased to provide the support needed to produce a new edition of this informative publication.

Those strong links have been forged not only as a result of our being its bankers but also through the active involvement of a number of our senior executives. Indeed some have continued that involvement into retirement.

As Britain's biggest bank, Barclays seek to promote the well-being of the community. Our efforts take many forms – such as our support for this book – and we like to concentrate our resources in areas of special need.

We believe that as we make a profit *in* the community, it is right we should make efforts *for* the community and this year we will spend over £11 million on a wide ranging programme of support, including charitable donations, employment initiatives, support for the arts and youth activities.

But money is only part of the help which the bank gives. In fact, there are times when manpower is considerably more important than even finance – which is why the bank lays great stress on its secondment programme, under which it lends over 100 senior members of staff each year to lead or help in a variety of community projects. This has been a further way in which the bank has worked alongside Age Concern in recent years.

Another major area for our support is the pioneering Barclays Youth Action Scheme which encourages young people to become actively involved in improving the environment in their local communities, while developing their own organisation and leadership skills. Since the scheme was launched in 1986, over £1 million has been awarded to such projects as voluntary help for disabled and elderly people and a wide variety of conservation efforts.

We believe working in partnership with such dedicated organisations as Age Concern emphasises our own commitment to the community and we wish the work every success for the future.

Brian Carr
Head of Barclays Bank
Community Enterprise Department

ABOUT THE AUTHORS

'Your Taxes' has been written by Sally West who is the Income Maintenance Information and Policy Officer at Age Concern England. She is also the author of *Your Rights: A Guide to Money Benefits for Older People*, also published by Age Concern England.

'Your Savings and Investments' and 'Other Financial Options' have been written by Jennie Hawthorne, a financial journalist. Her work has featured in most national newspapers, including *The Sunday Times, The Sunday Telegraph, The Observer, The Guardian, The Times, The Daily Telegraph, Daily Mail* and in numerous magazines. Formerly a Senior Lecturer in Economics and Monetary Theory, she has appeared on TV and radio, written several books of general interest, as well as academic texts and fiction.

INTRODUCTION

Over the past ten years the stock market has witnessed changeable conditions. The 'bull market' in the mid-1980s was followed by the stock market crash of 1987, and subsequent low levels of turnover and depressed market conditions. Inflation and high interest rates kept the market in a cautious mood for some time. More recently the resolution of the Gulf crisis has led to increased market volatility with the April 1991 *Financial Times* Stock Exchange 100 Index (based on the share performance of the UK's leading companies) reaching an all-time high.

Against this background the number of private investors has increased significantly over the last decade - more than 11 million people (25 per cent of the adult population) are shareholders. However, only a small proportion of them have invested in more than one company, and the proportion of shares owned by them has declined in contrast to those held by institutional investors such as pension funds.

This situation needs to be reversed with wider and deeper individual share ownership encouraged. People should be encouraged to hold equities as part of an investment portfolio alongside the more traditional types of saving media and collective investments such as unit trusts. Any reasonably long-term view of the financial markets shows that investing in the stock market brings a greater return than that gained from bank deposit accounts, building society savings and gilts, although of course there is some risk.

However, some people who can afford to take a longer term

view when considering investing in shares may be discouraged from doing so because of the restrictions of Capital Gains Tax. An important incentive in encouraging individual share investment would be the reform of CGT.

At present, as a shareholder, you would be liable to this tax on any profit made beyond the Capital Gains Tax threshold, currrently £5,500, when selling shares regardless of whether you reinvested promptly in another equity. It is not surprising that many prudent investors hold their shares through collective investment schemes where portfolio adjustments can be made without the CGT liability.

I suggest that simplification of the existing Capital Gains Tax regime would encourage private investors to hold shares directly, as they would be able to sell certain shares and buy into others without becoming liable for CGT, provided of course that the proceeds of such a switch were not used for spending. If any gain from the sale were actually withdrawn from the share portfolio, then tax would be payable on the gain, albeit in proportion to the overall appreciation in the value of the portfolio.

This 'holdover relief' should also make it possible for people to withdraw from a unit trust, for example, and transfer the proceeds directly into equities without incurring any liability of Capital Gains Tax. Furthermore, financial advisers could easily provide investors with a statement of CGT with their regular portfolio valuations.

Also essential in encouraging individual share ownership is accurate information about investments explained simply and clearly. Publications such as *Your Taxes and Savings* play an invaluable educational role - informing people about the principles involved and the many investment opportunities now available.

Andrew Hugh Smith
Chairman
London Stock Exchange

Your Taxes

This part of the book explains about tax and how your tax bill is worked out. In addition there are explanations of the tax allowances to which you may be entitled and some examples of how to calculate the tax you pay. The changes announced in recent Budgets are explained and incorporated in these illustrations – for example, Independent Taxation of married couples and the rules which now enable non-taxpayers to receive bank and building society interest free of tax.

There is a guide to who does what at the Inland Revenue and the best way to approach them. For further information about certain subjects, there are details about Inland Revenue leaflets, available free from local tax offices.

HOW THE TAX SYSTEM WORKS

The Inland Revenue is the Government department which deals with the main UK taxes. The people who represent it are: Collectors of Taxes who collect taxes and send out demands for arrears, and Inspectors of Taxes who assess the amount of tax you pay and deal with related problems. The Collector's and the Inspector's offices may be in different buildings or towns.

Which tax office handles your affairs will depend on your circumstances. If you are still in paid work, this will be your employer's tax office; if you are self-employed, this will be the office covering your business; and if you are unemployed or retired, this will be your last employer's tax office. New claims tax offices are being set up to deal with married women who require repayments because of the new independent tax legislation.

If you need general advice on Income Tax or Capital Gains Tax, you can contact a tax enquiry centre. Collection offices, tax offices and enquiry centres are listed in the phone book under 'Inland Revenue'.

Help the Inland Revenue staff and yourself by telling them all relevant information and quoting your Tax Reference Number and/or National Insurance Number which appears on any official communications sent to you. Always keep notices you receive from the Inland Revenue and copies of anything you send to them.

There are three main UK taxes for individuals assessed on an annual basis according to the 'tax year' which runs from 6 April in one year to 5 April in the following year.

o Income Tax paid on what you earn or receive as a pension or from investments;

o Capital Gains Tax paid on profits made when you sell an asset or give it away;

o Inheritance Tax paid on what you leave when you die and sometimes on a gift made in the seven years before you die.

■ Note that the Community Charge (sometimes called the Poll Tax) is dealt with by the local authority rather than the Inland Revenue. For details about the Community Charge system and recent changes, write to Age Concern England for factsheet No 21 (see page 119 for details).

Income Tax

This section gives details about how to calculate your Income Tax for the year 6 April 1991 to 5 April 1992.

To check whether you have to pay Income Tax and if so, how much for each tax year, you make certain calculations, as listed below.

1 Add together your different types of taxable income for the tax year (see pages 15–18).

2 Deduct allowances from this total, as everyone is entitled to some tax-free income (see pages 19–25).

3 Use the rates for the tax year to work out the amount of tax to be paid on what is left. Generally if your income is less than £23,700 after deducting allowances, you are a basic-rate taxpayer; if it is more than that, you are a higher-rate taxpayer.

Taxable Income	Rate of Tax
Up to £23,700	25 per cent
Over £23,700	40 per cent

INDEPENDENT TAXATION

In April 1990 Independent Taxation replaced the old system which regarded a married woman's income as if it were her husband's. Before then a husband and wife were generally treated as one person for tax purposes – now they are treated as separate taxpayers. This means their income is no longer added together, they each have their own allowances and are responsible for filling in their own tax returns. A married woman now does not have to tell her husband how much she earns or what savings she has. For more information about the allowances, see pages 19–25.

YOUR INCOME

Depending on your personal circumstances, you won't necessarily have to pay tax on all types of income. This section lists the main types of tax-free income, explains what income is taxable and how and when it is taxed.

Tax-free income

The main types of tax-free income that affect older people are listed below:

- Housing Benefit and Community Charge Benefit;
- Income Support for people aged 60 or over (and those who receive this without needing to be available for work);
- Invalidity Pension;
- Attendance Allowance;
- Mobility Allowance;
- Christmas Bonus for pensioners;
- industrial injury social security benefits;
- disablement pensions from the armed forces, police, fire brigade, merchant navy;
- additional payments to holders of gallantry awards;
- additions for dependent children;
- War Widow's Pension and allowances;
- pension annuities payable by Austria and West Germany to the victims of Nazi persecution;
- proceeds from National Savings certificates; first £70.00 interest from a National Savings Ordinary Account;
- gifts.

LEAVING OR REDUNDANCY PAYMENTS

The first £30,000 of leaving or redundancy payments or pay in lieu of notice will be tax free. Any excess, and all amounts to which you are entitled under your contract of employment, will be taxable in full. Your employer should deduct tax from the taxable amount under PAYE.

Some leaving payments may be completely tax free – for example, a lump sum for an injury or disability that has meant you can no longer continue with employment or a payment on leaving a job where you mainly worked abroad.

If you decide to retire early, you may get a refund of contributions paid into your employer's pension scheme if you have less than two years' service with the organisation. Tax at 20 per cent is usually deducted from the refund before it is paid to you.

How income is taxed

PAY AS YOU EARN (PAYE)

Tax on earnings and any occupational pension is generally collected through the PAYE system. Under this, your tax allowances are divided up as weekly or monthly amounts and deducted from your pension and/or earnings each week or month before tax is charged. Everyone who is taxed under PAYE has a code which enables their employer to deduct the right amount (see also pages 33–35).

PENSIONS

The State Pension is taxable but, if it is your only income, you will not usually have to pay tax because your allowances will probably be higher. If your State Pension plus any other taxable income comes to more than your allowances, you will be liable for tax.

■ Note that the total State Pension a married woman receives, whether based on her own or her husband's contributions, now counts as her income under Independent Taxation. However, if you receive extra pension for your spouse which is paid with your pension (known as the Adult Dependency Increase), this will be taxed as part of *your* pension.

Example
Mr Patel is 65 and receives an addition of £31.25 for his wife who is 59 and does not work. This is taxed as his income.

Once she becomes 60, she can draw the married woman's pension of £31.25 which is paid to her and taxed as part of her income.

If you get a pension from an ex-employer and/or a private pension, the tax to be paid on your combined State, occupational and private pensions is normally deducted from your occupational pension through the PAYE system. It may look as though you are being taxed at a very high rate on the occupational pension; but when you realise that the tax on your State or private pension is being taken care of too, it makes more sense. You may qualify for an extra 10 per cent allowance against a pension received from abroad. The Inspector may have to make a separate assessment to collect tax on this source of income.

EARNINGS

If you retire (from a job) without a pension, be sure to collect your P45 form to pass on to your new employer. This tells the employer which code to use to ensure that you pay the right amount of tax on earnings and the State Pension. Until your employer has your P45, showing your correct tax code, any earnings from a job will be taxed on the emergency code which for 1991-92 is 329L (see also pages 33–35 for information about your tax code and PAYE).

If you have a pension from a previous employer and you get another job, your new employer will ask you to sign form P46 and will give you a form P15 (allowances claim) so that the right PAYE code can be given for taxing your earnings. This is necessary because in these circumstances there will not be a P45.

INVESTMENT INCOME

This section gives information about the taxation of income from savings and investments. Some savings, for example, most National Savings accounts pay income gross — that is, without the deduction of any tax. Income from other investments is paid with tax already deducted. Since April 1991 there have been changes to the way interest from bank and building society accounts is taxed, as explained below.

Bank and building society accounts

Before April 1991, interest from bank and building society accounts was paid after deduction of the 'composite' rate of tax. Non-taxpayers could not claim back this tax. However, from 6 April 1991, this system of composite rate tax has been abolished.

Now, non-taxpayers can receive interest from bank and building society accounts gross – that is, without deduction of any tax. Other people will receive interest with basic-rate tax already deducted. If you expect your total gross income (including gross income from accounts) to be less than your tax allowance(s), you can apply to have the interest paid gross by completing form R85. A husband and wife who are both non-taxpayers will each need to complete a form.

If you are a non-taxpayer but do not apply for bank or building society interest to be paid gross or you are due to pay tax on some, but not all, of your interest, you can apply for a refund of any tax overpaid at the end of the tax year.

If you are a taxpayer, the 'grossed-up' interest will be included to check whether you qualify for the full Age Allowance, as explained below. If you are a higher-rate taxpayer, you may be liable for further tax.

Investment income with tax deducted

Other types of investment income, including dividends from shares in UK companies and distributions from unit trusts, are paid with basic-rate tax deducted. However, if you are a non-taxpayer or you should have paid less tax overall, you can claim back overpaid tax (see page 37).

If tax has already been deducted and you are a basic-rate taxpayer, you will not have to pay any more tax; but if you are a higher-rate taxpayer, you will be liable for the extra tax. Income paid with tax deducted is 'grossed up' to check whether you will qualify for the full Age Allowance.

Income paid net of basic-rate tax is taken into account when calculating your total income to determine whether you are entitled to the higher allowances for your age group. The 'gross' amount is included (ie as if no tax had been deducted) so every £75.00 of interest you receive (already taxed) is treated by the tax office as £100 before tax has been deducted.

You will not pay tax twice on savings account interest, but the gross amount must be included in your total income when calculating your allowance. If gross income is more than £13,500, the higher allowances for people aged 65 or over are reduced, as explained on pages 20-21.

When tax is paid

With some types of investment, including National Savings ordinary and investment accounts, the amount credited to you in the previous tax year is normally used in calculating your tax for the year. So, for your 1991-92 bill, your income for 1990-91 will be used. Tax owed on these forms of investment will normally be due on 1 January in the tax year. However, if the amount of interest is small, it may be collected under PAYE. Income from other investments (ie dividends and bank and building society interest) is used to work out your tax bill for the tax year during which you receive the income.

If you are a higher-rate taxpayer and extra tax is due on interest you have received net, you will probably have to pay it in a lump sum on 1 December, following the tax year. If you have a consistent source of income which is paid gross, you may be able to arrange the collection of tax by PAYE or offset the amount due (if it is small) against your Personal Allowance.

For more information, see the leaflets *Can you stop paying tax on your bank and building society interest?* (IR 110) and *How to reclaim a repayment of tax on bank and building society interest* (IR 111).

YOUR ALLOWANCES

Everyone is entitled to a personal tax allowance and many people receive other allowances as well. These reduce the amount of income on which tax is paid. This section of the book explains the allowances for the 1991–92 tax year (including those which were replaced in April 1990).

Allowances before April 1990

The introduction of Independent Taxation brought about the following changes:

- The Single Person's Allowance, Age Allowance and the Married Man's Allowance were replaced by the Personal Allowance and the Married Couple's Allowance. These two new allowances are both higher for people aged 65 and over, as explained below.

- The Wife's Earned Income Allowance no longer exists, as married women now have their own Personal Allowance instead.

  ■ While many older couples benefited or were unaffected by Independent Taxation, some couples were left worse off by the new allowances. These people may be able to receive help through the transitional arrangements described on page 21.

Allowances under Independent Taxation

The main difference under the new system is that a married woman can claim her own Personal Allowance to set against her income including investments or a State Pension based on her own or her husband's contributions. If a couple own assets jointly, each will normally be taxed on half of the income, unless they have informed the Inland Revenue that the income is split differently.

PERSONAL ALLOWANCE

This is available to everyone – men, women, married or single – and is paid at three different levels depending on your age and, for people aged 65 or over, your income (see below):

- o £3,295 for people aged under 65;
- o £4,020 for people aged between 65 and 74;
- o £4,180 for people aged 75 and over.

You can claim the higher levels of Personal Allowance for a whole tax year (6 April to 5 April) if you turn 65 or 75 at any time during the year. So, even if your birthday is on 5 April (at the end of the tax year), you can claim for the whole of that tax year. Give the Inland Revenue your date of birth so that they give you the right Personal Allowance. However, do note that the Personal Allowance cannot be transferred between husband and wife (see below).

The higher allowances for those aged 65 or more will be reduced if income is above £13,500, but it will not be reduced to less than the basic Personal Allowance paid to those under 65. For every £2.00 of extra income above £13,500, your allowance will be reduced by £1.00. When your income reaches £14,950 or more (if you are aged 65 to 74) and £15,270 or more (if you are aged 75 or more), the allowance will be reduced to the basic Personal Allowance.

This income limit now applies separately to the income of both a husband and wife, whereas in the past it applied to their combined income.

MARRIED COUPLE'S ALLOWANCE

A married man living with his wife can claim the full Married Couple's Allowance, provided their marriage took place before 6 May in the tax year concerned. If they married after this date, the man will receive a reduced amount.

If as a married man, your income is not high enough to use all or any of the Married Couple's Allowance, the unused part can be transferred to your wife. You must contact your tax office and ask for the unused part of your allowance to be transferred. Note that you cannot transfer your Personal Allowance.

There are three different levels for the Married Couple's Allowance depending on how old you (or your spouse) are during the tax year and subject to an income limit for people aged 65 or over.

o £1,720 if both of you are under 65;

o £2,355 if either of you are 65 or over;

o £2,395 if either of you are 75 or over.

The Married Couple's Allowance for people aged 65 or over will be reduced by £1.00 for every £2.00 by which the husband's income exceeds a certain limit. If a married man of 65 or over has an income of more than £13,500, this will first reduce his Personal Allowance; then if it is high enough, it will reduce the Married Couple's Allowance.

A married man aged 65 to 74 with a wife under 75 will have his Personal Allowance and the Married Couple's Allowance reduced to the level of someone under 65 if his income is more than £16,220. For a married man aged 75 or over, these allowances will be reduced to the level of a married man under 65 when his income reaches £16,620.

Transitional arrangements

In certain situations Independent Taxation, as explained on page 13, may leave some couples worse off. The transitional reliefs outlined below were introduced to phase in the new system for these people. The amount of any transitional relief depends on an individual's circumstances. Only brief details are given here, so contact your tax office for further information.

SPECIAL PERSONAL ALLOWANCE

If a couple qualified for the Age Allowance in the 1989–90 tax year because of the wife's age, under Independent Taxation their allowances may be lower. This is because in the past the Married Man's Allowance was increased, whereas now only the Married Couple's Allowance is increased – not the husband's Personal Allowance too. Some married men in this position may qualify for a special personal allowance as long as it was also due in 1990- 91.

HUSBANDS ON A LOW INCOME

Under the old system of taxation if a husband's income was less than his total allowances, he could transfer any unused allowances to his wife. Under Independent Taxation only the Married Couple's Allowance can be transferred.

After transferring the unused portion of the Married Couple's Allowance, a married man's income may still be less than his allowances. If this is the case, his wife may be entitled to a transitional allowance if she received a transitional allowance in 1990–91.

MARRIED COUPLE'S ALLOWANCE

A married man who is separated from his wife at the start of the tax year will not normally be able to receive the Married Couple's Allowance, whereas under the old system, in some circumstances, he may have been able to continue claiming the Married Man's Allowance. This transitional allowance may be given to a man separated from his wife before 6 April 1990 who is still married to her and wholly maintaining her with voluntary payments.

For further information, see the following leaflets: *A Guide for Married Couples* (IR 80); *A Guide for Pensioners* (IR 81); *A Guide for Husbands on a Low Income* (IR 82); *A Guide to Tax Allowances and Reliefs* (IR 90).

Other allowances

You may get extra relief if you qualify for any of the allowances outlined below.

Additional personal allowance

- An extra allowance of £1,720 a year can be claimed by certain individuals who have a 'qualifying child' resident with them for the whole or part of the year. These include a single person bringing up children. By adding £1,720 to the Personal Allowance, a single parent aged under 65 will receive the same total allowances as a married man.

  A 'qualifying child' includes those under 16 and, broadly speaking, those who are older provided that they are in full-time education or are undergoing certain types of training.

- A married man whose wife is totally incapacitated can also claim the same allowance of £1,720 on top of his Married Couple's Allowance.

Blind person's allowance

Provided you are registered as blind with a local authority, you can claim an allowance of £1,080 at any time in the tax year. If both husband and wife are registered as blind, they will each receive an allowance of £1,080.

For a couple, if either partner has an income too small to use up all their allowance, the unused portion can be transferred to the other partner who does not have to be blind.

You may be able to register as blind, even though you are not totally without sight. To be registered, you must show your lack of sight makes it impossible to perform any work for which eyesight is essential. You do not, however, get the Blind Person's Allowance if you are registered with your local authority as partially sighted.

Private medical insurance

For certain private medical insurance policies, for people aged 60 and over, tax relief is available on premiums paid. For basic-rate taxpayers the premiums will be adjusted accordingly by the insurance company, while higher-rate taxpayers will have to claim their extra relief on their tax return. Tax relief is also available for people who pay private medical insurance premiums for someone else who is aged 60 or over.

To be eligible for tax relief the policy must not pay out more than £5.00 a night in cash benefits. This could exclude many 'waiting list' policies which pay out larger sums if you are treated under the NHS. For a joint policy at least one person must be 60 or over for it to qualify for tax relief. Policies that cover dependent children are not eligible for tax relief.

LIFE ASSURANCE

Tax relief of 12.5 per cent is given on premiums on a qualifying life assurance policy taken out on or before 13 March 1984. The tax relief is given directly to the insurance company concerned and not to the policy holder, who pays the net premium to the company. On a policy taken out after that date, there is no tax relief on premiums – unless it is attached to a Self-Employed Pension Contract. This is called a Section 226A policy, which earns tax relief up to the highest rate.

■ Do note that since June 1988 no new Section 226A policies have been available (see also page 101).

MAINTENANCE PAYMENTS

If you make maintenance payments to a divorced or separated spouse under court orders or legally binding agreements made since 15 March 1988, you get tax relief up to maximum of £1,720 for the 1991–92 tax year. Voluntary payments and those paid directly to children do not attract tax relief. If you receive maintenance payments under these rules, you do not have to pay tax on the payments.

Special rules apply to agreements and court orders made prior to 15 March 1988, and, in certain cases, to court orders made and agreements notified to the tax office by 30 June 1988.

WIDOW'S BEREAVEMENT

If you are a widow you will qualify for an allowance of £1,720 to be set against your income from the date of your bereavement to the end of the tax year, as long as your husband was entitled to the Married Couple's Allowance. You can also receive the allowance in the tax year following the one when your husband died provided you have not remarried before the start of the year.

WIDOWS AND WIDOWERS

In the year when a man becomes a widower, he can claim the full Married Couple's Allowance for the whole year, even though his wife died part way through the tax year.

In the year when a woman becomes a widow, she can claim the following allowances:

o a Personal Allowance;

o any of the Married Couple's Allowance which is unused at the time of her husband's death (the husband's executors can ask for this to be transferred).

o the Widow's Bereavement Allowance, as described above.

Example

Sophie is 60 and her husband, Bob, died aged 70 at the end of April 1991. Up until then their incomes were assessed separately and they qualified for Personal Allowances of £3,295 and £4,020 respectively. Bob also qualified for the Higher Married Couple's Allowance of £2,355.

After Bob's death Sophie told her tax office about her changed circumstances. Sophie continues with her Personal Allowance of £3,295 and gains any unused part of the Married Couple's Allowance. She also gets the Widow's Bereavement Allowance of £1,720 to set against her income for all of the tax year. If she does not remarry before the start off the next tax year, she will receive her Personal Allowance plus the Widow's Bereavement Allowance and in subsequent years, just her Personal Allowance.

For further information about Independent Taxation, see the following leaflets: *Tax Relief for Private Medical Insurance* (IR103); *A Guide for Widows and Widowers* (IR91); *A Guide for One-Parent Families* (IR92); *Income Tax- A Guide to Separation, Divorce and Maintenance Payments* (IR93).

Claiming for previous years

If you have not claimed an allowance in previous years and you think you may have been entitled to it, all is not lost. You can claim back for six years, as well as for the current year. Write to your tax office saying when you think you first became entitled to the allowance and giving all the details necessary. If your claim is accepted, you will get a rebate for any overpaid tax and you may get some extra to compensate for a late payment, called a repayment supplement.

If you think the Inland Revenue have made a mistake on your allowances, see page 38.

HOW TO CHECK YOUR TAX BILL

This section of the book shows you how to check that you have paid the right amount of Income Tax.

Follow the steps outlined below and refer to the preceding sections where necessary.

1 List all sources of income for the year and add up what you received, bearing in mind that for some investment income you include what you received in the previous year (see pp 15–18).

2 List the allowances to which you are entitled (see pp 19–25), and add them together.

3 Deduct the total allowances from the total income to get the amount of your taxable income.

4 Work out the tax you should pay by taking 25 per cent of your taxable income up to £23,700 and 40 per cent of anything over that amount and adding the two figures together.

5 Compare this figure to that on your Notice of Assessment, if you receive one (see p 36). For how to check your PAYE payments and what to do if you think there is an error in your bill, see pp 33–35.

The examples which follow illustrate some typical situations and should clarify how the Inland Revenue works out your bill and how you can check it.

A single person

Example

Joan (aged 77) is retired and gets the State Pension and a pension from her former employer. In addition she receives interest from National Savings ordinary and investment accounts. Joan follows the steps from page 27 to work out her tax for the 1991–92 tax year.

Step 1. **Joan** received £50.00 interest in 1990–91 on her ordinary account. As this is less than £70.00, it will be tax-free (see p 14). Her taxable sources of income are added together as follows:

State Pension	£2,704.00
Pension from employer	£1,000.00
Interest from National Savings investment account	£300.00
Total Income	**£4,004.00**

Step 2. As Joan is over 75 she is entitled to the highest Personal Allowance. As her total income is less than £13,500, she can claim the full higher allowance.

Personal Allowance	£4,180.00
Total Allowances	**£4,180.00**

Step 3. Joan's taxable income of £4,004 is less than her Personal Allowance of £4,180.

Step 4. Joan is not liable for income tax because her income is less than her allowance.

A married couple

Example

Clive is 68 and married to Lorna who is 63. Their tax positions are considered separately.

Step 1. **Clive** has retired and receives the State Pension and a pension from his last employer. He and Lorna have a joint National Savings investment account on which they had interest of £400.00 for 1990–91. The Inland Revenue will treat this as being split equally between them, which amounts to £200.00 each. Clive works out his total income.

State Pension	£2,704.00
Pension from employer	£6,000.00
Interest from National Savings investment account	£200.00
Total Income	£8,904.00

Step 2. Clive is entitled to the following higher allowances (because his total income is below £13,500, he will receive the full age allowances):

Personal Allowance (65 to 74)	£4,020.00
Married Couple's Allowance (65 to 74)	£2,355.00
Total Allowances	£6,375.00

Step 3. Clive's taxable income is £8,904 less £6,375 which gives £2,529.

Step 4. Clive's tax bill is 25 per cent of £2,529 (as it falls within the basic-rate band) which is £632.25. The tax on his pensions will have been deducted from his occupational pension, so he will just owe the tax on his National Savings Account (unless this has already been included in his PAYE code).

Turn to page 30 to see how Lorna works out her tax bill.

Step 1. **Lorna** has recently retired from full-time work but does not get a pension from her former employer. In addition to the State Pension, she receives earnings from a part-time job and £300.00 in dividends during the 1991–92 tax year. She adds up her taxable income.

State Pension	£2,704.00
Earnings	£2,000.00
Interest from National Savings investment account	£200.00
Dividends (gross)	£400.00
Total Income	£5,304.00

Step 2. She is only entitled to the basic Personal Allowance:

Total Allowances £3,295.00

Step 3. Lorna's total taxable income is £5,304 less £3,295 which gives £2,009.

Step 4. Lorna's tax bill will be 25 per cent of £2,009 which is £502.25. The tax on her State Pension and her earnings is paid through PAYE. The income from dividends will be paid with the tax already deducted, so there is only the tax on her interest left to pay (unless this has already been included in her PAYE code).

Married couple with investment income

Example

■ Note that under Independent Taxation a married woman's investment income will be taxed as her own. A couple may be able to save tax if investments in the husband's name are moved to the wife to use her allowances or to enable them to pay tax at a lower rate.

Sid and Lilian are both 65. In 1991–92 Sid receives the State Pension, a private pension and interest from a building society account. Lilian receives only the married woman's State Pension of £1,625. This is less than her Personal Allowance of £4,020, so she pays no tax. Sid works out his tax bill as follows.

State Pension	£2,704.00
Private pension	£9,000.00
Building society interest (gross)	£2,000.00
Total Income	£13,704.00
Personal Allowance (65 to 74)	£4,020.00
Married Couple's Allowance (65 to 74)	£2,355.00
Total Allowances	£6,375.00

Sid's gross income of £13,704 is more than the income limit of £13,500. Because his income is £204 above the income limit, his Personal Allowance is reduced by £102 (£1.00 for every £2.00), so his total allowance will be £6,273.

Sid's taxable income is £13,704 less £6,273 which gives £7,431. This will be taxed at 25 per cent, so his total tax bill will be £1,857.75. Tax on Sid's pensions was paid through PAYE, and the building society interest had basic-rate tax deducted. However, he will still owe a little more tax unless his PAYE code took into account his reduced Personal Allowance.

Sid and Lillian's total bill could have been reduced if Sid had transferred his building society account to Lillian before the start of the tax year. Lillian's income would then have consisted of the State Pension of £1,625 plus the interest of £2,000, making a total of £3,625. She would still have been a non-taxpayer, and could have applied to have the interest paid without tax deducted. Sid's total income would have been £11,704, so he would have received his full Personal Allowance.

USING TAX FORMS

There are a number of official forms that may be sent to you in connection with your tax affairs. This section looks at the main pieces of paperwork and what they mean.

Notice of Coding

The Notice of Coding shows how your PAYE code is calculated and, if you work, tells your employer what that code is. The employer uses the code to deduct approximately the right amount of tax from your pay or occupational pension.

The number in your tax code is the tax-free income you are allowed with the last digit removed. The higher your PAYE code, the less tax you pay. The lower the number, the more tax you pay. The letters used in the codes are explained below.

- L means that you get the basic Personal Allowance.

- H means that you get an allowance equal to the Personal Allowance plus either the Additional Personal Allowance or the basic Married Couple's Allowance.

- P means that you get the higher Personal Allowance for a single person who is aged between 65 and 74.

- V means that you get both the higher Personal and Married Couple's Allowances and you are aged between 65 and 74.

- T means that none of the other code letters apply. It may be given if your age-related Personal Allowance is reduced (because your income is above the income limit, for example) or you get the higher Personal Allowance because you are 75 or over. This code letter can be used if you do not want your employer to know which tax allowances you receive.

- F means that your State Pension and other benefits are greater than the allowances to which you are entitled. You will be taxed a higher than normal rate on the whole amount of an occupational pension and on earnings. If this did not happen, you might owe tax at the end of the tax year.

Tax is deducted at a higher rate from your occupational pension or earnings because your State Pension also has to be taken into account. If you are given an F code, you will still receive your full allowance(s), so over all – provided you are a basic-rate taxpayer – you will still be paying tax at 25 per cent. The number in an F code simply indicates to any employer at what rate tax should be deducted from your earnings.

- NT means that you pay no tax on what you earn.

- OT means that all your earnings are to be taxed – ie you have no free-of-tax amount.

- D means that you have a second job and that your taxable income is large enough to pay tax at the higher rate. If your taxable income is below £23,700 for the 1991–92 tax year, you should not have this code.

- BR means that tax is collected at the basic rate on a second job.

CHECKING YOUR NOTICE OF CODING

If you receive the State Pension as well as an occupational pension and other income, you will get a Notice of Coding before 6 April – the start of the tax year. This will show your code with a deduction for the State Pension at the rate in force at the beginning of the tax year. Some people may get a further Notice of Coding after the Budget in March. Most codes will be increased automatically by your employer to take account of the Budget changes, on instructions from the Inland Revenue.

If you do not get a new code for the start of the new tax year on 6 April, your pay or pension office will continue with the code being used up to 5 April (the last day of the old tax year).

When you get a new Notice of Coding, check whether:

o you have been given the correct allowances (the amounts for the coming tax year announced in the Budget);

o the deductions for the State Pension and any untaxed investment income are correct;

o the addition and subtraction are right;

o the code letter is the appropriate one for your circumstances.

When checking your PAYE code note the following: if your code has gone up, you will be paying less tax; if it has gone down, you will be paying more. If you disagree with anything on the Notice of Coding, take a copy of it and send the original back to the tax office, saying what you think is wrong.

There may be other changes in your circumstances which affect your PAYE code (apart from a change in the State pension, for which the tax office adjusts your code automatically). These changes could be:

o getting married;

o giving up work;

o death of your spouse;

o separation or divorce;

o starting work or becoming self-employed;

o becoming entitled to an additional allowance or losing the right to one.

It is up to you to inform the tax office of any changes in your circumstances which might affect your code and the amount of tax you pay.

See leaflet *Income Tax – PAYE* (IR 34).

The tax return

If you are self-employed or a higher-rate taxpayer, you will usually be sent a tax return every year. If you pay tax through PAYE and your tax affairs are straightforward, you probably will not be sent one.

The tax return deals with two tax years. Part of it looks back to your income, outgoings and capital gains during the past tax year. The other part looks forward to the future tax year, starting on 6 April, so that the tax office can decide which allowances you will qualify for. If you receive a tax return, fill it in carefully and return it within 30 days. If you cannot meet this deadline, inform your tax office.

There are different tax returns for different sorts of taxpayers. The main types are:

o form P1 – a blue form, mainly for people with straightforward tax affairs whose income is less than £8,500 a year;

o form 11P – a brown form, for people whose income is more than £8,500 a year or who have more complex tax affairs;

o form 11 – a blue form, mainly for self-employed people;

Notice of Assessment

This sets out your tax bill for the year and shows how the Inland Revenue have worked it out. However, if you are an employee and pay tax under PAYE, you are unlikely to receive a Notice of Assessment. If you do not agree with the amounts on the form, appeal in writing within 30 days of the date on it.

You may receive a Notice of Assessment if you:

o filled in a tax return and there was something not taken account of in your PAYE code;

o pay tax at the higher rate;

o have income from a number of sources;

o are being sent a rebate of overpaid tax;

o have underpaid tax in the past.

CLAIMING A TAX REBATE

If the State Pension is your only income when you retire, send your P45 form to your tax office, including details of age, the date you retired and your estimated total income for the rest of the tax year (ie from the day you retire until the next 5 April). If any refund is due, it will come directly from the tax office.

If you get a pension from an ex-employer, any rebate due for the tax year in which you retired will be paid via the pension you receive from your ex-employer – but only after the employer receives notification from the tax office of the proper code. If this information is not received by the end of the tax year when you retired, any rebate would come direct from the tax office.

If you have a personal pension, send your P45 form to the officials operating the fund. Any rebate due will be added to the amount of your pension.

If you have paid tax on investment income such as dividends or distributions from a unit trust, and you have not used up all of your tax allowances, you can apply for a repayment. If the total amount overpaid is £50.00 or less, you should apply at the end of the tax year; but if it is over £50.00, you may be able to receive a repayment during the year.

If you already make a claim each year, you should receive claim form R40 as usual. Remember to include the certificate you get showing the amount of tax deducted with your claim for repayment. If you have not previously claimed back tax, complete form R95 (D) attached to leaflet IR 112 *How to claim a repayment of Income Tax.* For more information about claiming back tax overpaid on bank and building society accounts, see page 17.

OFFICIAL ERROR CONCESSION

If the Inland Revenue makes a mistake and later discovers that you have not paid enough tax, you may not have to pay the difference. This depends on whether your income falls within certain limits when you are first notified of the extra tax due.

If the Inland Revenue fails to act on information you have supplied, in writing, in a reasonable time and if you believe that your tax affairs were in order, then you could qualify for the Official Error Concession.

At the time of writing, if your income before tax is not above £12,000 a year, and other criteria are satisfied, none of the tax owed as a result of the tax office error will be collected. The proportion of arrears collected increases until your income is above £32,000 when all the arrears are collected.

If you are 65 or over, or are receiving a State Retirement or Widow's Pension, all the limits are increased by £3,000. So you could, for example, have an income of up to £15,300 and not have to pay any tax owed.

Owing tax from previous years

There may be another reason why you have not paid enough tax – due to an oversight – and there could be back tax to pay. If you think that you may have taxable income which has not been reported, go to your nearest tax office and explain. The Inland Revenue can go back any length of time to examine the rate of tax paid and your income.

Of course, people who have deliberately evaded tax are liable to penalties.

CAPITAL GAINS TAX

You may have to pay some Capital Gains Tax (CGT) if you sell or give away an asset such as shares, or in some cases, a house. After taking into account expenses and the effect of inflation, you may have to pay tax if you have made a profit or if the asset has increased in value.

How it is calculated

The cost or value of the asset when you acquired it – and, in some cases related expenses – is adjusted for inflation using the Retail Prices Index (RPI), which is the Government's measure of how prices are rising (also called indexation). The 'indexed' value of an asset is deducted from the selling price or its market value (if you gave it away or sold it for less than market value). If deducting the indexed value leaves a positive figure, you have made a gain on which you may have to pay tax. If it results in a negative figure, this is an allowable loss.

Before Capital Gains Tax comes into effect, you are allowed to make a certain amount of profit – £5,500 for 1991–92 (increased from £5,000 in 1990–91). Anything above that amount is taxed at 25 or 40 per cent, depending on whether you are a basic or higher-rate taxpayer. Under Independent Taxation a husband and wife will be taxed independently on any gains, and each partner will be entitled to a separate exempt amount.

The gains and losses made when selling an asset can be 'netted off', which means that if the net gain is less than £5,500, there will be no CGT to pay. If the net gain is over the tax-free amount of £5,500 to which everybody is entitled, you must add the excess to your income to see at what rate the gain will be taxed.

Example
If you bought some shares in February 1989 for £10,000 and sold them in December 1990 for £17,000, you would work out the capital gain as outlined below. However, note that this

example looks at gains made in the year 1990–91. In the current tax year (1991–92) the annual exemption is £5,500.

1 Take the RPI for December 1990, 129.9, and divide it by the RPI for February 1989, 111.8. This gives 1.162 which shows how much prices have gone up between February 1989 and December 1990.

2 Multiply the cost of the shares, £10,000 by 1.162 to take inflation into account. This equals £11,620.

3 Deduct £11,620 from £17,000. This gives £5,380. As everyone is entitled to make gains of up to £5,000 a year (annual exemption in 1990–91) before having to pay CGT, the gain to be added to your taxable income would be £380.

■ Note that assets acquired before 31 March 1982 may involve slightly different calculations, and you should get further advice.

You should also be aware that some kinds of assets do not count towards the £5,500 gain you are allowed to make before CGT takes effect. They include:

o gifts between a co-habiting husband and wife;

o your only or main private residence (see below);

o private cars;

o British money;

o most British government stocks;

o personal belongings worth up to £6,000 each;

o proceeds of most life assurance policies;

o Premium Bond prizes, betting winnings;

o gifts to registered charities.

Capital Gains Tax will not usually be payable if and when you sell or give away the house you live in, provided it has been your 'main residence' throughout your ownership, has not been let, and the grounds do not exceed half a hectare (a bit more than one acre). However, if you give away or leave your house to someone, the recipient may have to pay CGT in the future when it is sold.

If you own two houses, you can nominate one of them to be your 'main residence'. The other may be exempt from CGT provided it is occupied by a dependent relative rent-free and was declared to the Inland Revenue by 5 April 1988.

Letting your home

If you let your home but do not live in it, when you come to sell it, the home will be assessed for CGT.

If you have a lodger in the home you own who shares a kitchen and bathroom and living space with you and is treated as a member of the family, you should not have to pay CGT when you sell the property.

However, if there is à more formal arrangement with the lodger, the rules may be different. If only a couple of rooms are rented, CGT will be calculated in proportion to the rented part and the period of letting relative to the total period of ownership.

Selling your business

If you sell all or part of your business after you are 55 (whether you retire or not), you may not have to pay CGT on up to £150,000 of the net gain *or* on more than half the net gain made between £150,000 and £600,000. The relief is determined by how long you owned the business. You may also be entitled to this relief if you are forced to retire early due to ill-health.

To qualify for tax relief on health grounds, you will have to satisfy the tax office that you have stopped working and are unable to do work of the kind you were previously doing because of ill-health and that you are likely to remain permanently unable to do work of that kind.

Selling your shares

Shares and unit trusts have CGT calculated when you sell them or give them away – usually in the same way as other assets. But when you sell or give away shares of the same type in the same company which you acquired at different times, there are special rules which govern the way gains and losses are worked out.

For more information, see Inland Revenue leaflets: *Capital Gains Tax and Owner-Occupied Houses* (CGT4); *Capital Gains Tax* (CGT8); *Retirement Relief on Disposal of a Business* (CGT6); *The Indexation Allowance for Quoted Shares* (CGT13)

INHERITANCE TAX

Inheritance Tax (IHT) may have to be paid on what you leave to your heirs or give away in the seven years before your death. However, no Inheritance Tax is likely to be payable on your estate provided you leave virtually everything to your spouse or you have a house or other assets now worth less than £140,000 and have made no recent large gifts. Note that a husband and wife each have their own IHT exemptions, and their own running total of chargeable gifts.

Under present rules your heirs will not have to pay tax on gifts received from you provided you live more than seven years after giving the gift. Whether or not you survive the seven years, the gift will not be taxed provided it is:

o a wedding gift of up to £5,000 to your child, or £2,500 to your grandchild or more remote descendant, or £1,000 to anyone else;

o a small gift not exceeding £250 per recipient per tax year;

o a regular gift out of income that does not reduce your standard of living;

o a gift made to a qualifying political party or to a United Kingdom registered charity.

There is an annual exemption of £3,000 for other gifts which are not covered in the above list (plus any unused balance of the previous year's exemption).

Inheritance Tax is dealt with by the Capital Taxes Office, as listed on page 114.

The calculations

To find out whether your heirs are likely to face a bill on your estate, do the following calculations.

- Add up the value of everything you own, including savings, investments and life assurance policies (unless these are written in trust).

- Add to the above total any gifts you have made in the past seven years, but do not include any gifts which are tax free (see above).

- Take away any money owed on your mortgage or any other debts. (When you die, unpaid bills, taxes, reasonable funeral expenses, etc will also be deducted before you are assessed for IHT).

- Take away from the total what you intend to leave to a spouse or to charity.

- Compare the total with the current threshold for IHT – £140,000 in the 1991–92 tax year. If your total is more than this, it is likely there will be IHT to pay. For a rough idea of how large the bill will be, calculate 40 per cent (the current rate of IHT) of the amount over the threshold.

Trusts and IHT planning

It is possible to plan ahead to cut any possible IHT bill by putting money into a trust, perhaps for your children or grandchildren. A trust is a legal document that allows you to give assets away, without actually giving those assets to a particular person at the time. Money paid into a trust is normally treated as separate from your estate and is taxed in a different (often complex) way.

■ Note that if you reserve a benefit from a gift you make, whether into a trust or not – for instance, by giving away your home and continuing to live in it – the gift will still count as part of your estate when you die. Such gifts are known as 'gifts with reservation'.

If you are thinking of setting up a trust, get professional advice from a solicitor or accountant. Find out whether the tax situation of the people who benefit from the trust will be affected and how much the setting up and administration of the trust will cost. Also the rules on taxing a trust are very complicated, and the solicitor or accountant who helps set up the trust should give you advice on this. If you have already established a trust, don't change what you are doing without taking professional advice.

Inheritance Tax provides a strong incentive for people who are really sure they can afford to make lifetime gifts to make them early. For people who own a home but do not have a great deal else to give away, the safest course is to make gifts within the exemption limit.

Tax avoidance schemes

Various insurance companies and financial consultants market plans to reduce or avoid Inheritance Tax. Such schemes can be complicated – involving juggling the ownership of money, making gifts from trusts, with the 'wealth-owner' taking out an insurance policy.

Before committing yourself to any scheme, be sure it has the approval of the Inland Revenue, and discuss it with your bank manager, solicitor or other professional adviser.

For more information see the Inland Revenue leaflet: *An Introduction to Inheritance Tax* (IHT3).

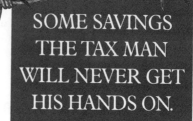

SOME SAVINGS THE TAX MAN WILL NEVER GET HIS HANDS ON.

Whether you pay income tax or not, we can show you a way to stop paying tax on your savings.

If you are a taxpayer, all you need do is open a Barclays TESSA (Tax Exempt Special Savings Account), which pays interest annually at an attractive 14%* tax free.

And if you don't pay income tax, there's no need to pay tax on your savings after April 6th.

Either way, there's nothing in it for the Inland Revenue.

If you'd like further information and an application form, phone the Barclays Information Line on 0800 400 100 free, or fill in the coupon.

You could soon be making savings on your savings.

Please send me details of how to stop paying tax on my savings.
Name (Mr/Mrs/Miss/Ms)_____ AC
Address_____

Postcode_____ Date_____
I would like information relating to:
Taxpayers ☐ Non-Taxpayers ☐
(Please tick box)

+ + + YOU'RE
BETTER OFF
TALKING TO

PLEASE RETURN THE COMPLETED COUPON TO:
BARCLAYS SAVINGS SERVICE, FREEPOST (GR 2199),
P.O. BOX 111, GLOUCESTER GL4 7RP. (No stamp required)

❀ BARCLAYS

CALL THE BARCLAYS INFORMATION LINE ON 0800 400 100 FREE

*INTEREST RATES MAY VARY AND ARE CORRECT AT TIME OF GOING TO PRESS. **TAX FREE** — THIS INDICATES THAT INTEREST IS EXEMPT FROM INCOME TAX, PROVIDED ALL TESSA CONDITIONS ARE MET. FULL DETAILS ARE AVAILABLE ON REQUEST.
REG. OFFICE: BARCLAYS BANK PLC, 54 LOMBARD STREET, LONDON EC3P 3AH. REG NO. 1026167.

ADVERTISEMENT

Your Savings and Investments

In this part of of the book, savings and investment opportunities are outlined for people of modest means and those fortunate enough to have upwards of £50,000 but no clear idea of how to invest it: how to get the best return from various bank and building society accounts as well as National Savings, Government stocks, shares, Personal Equity Plans, unit and investment trusts.

The principles to follow in getting the best value from your money are shown with examples of investment portfolios for both a single person and a married couple.

In addition, there is guidance on how to get unbiased financial advice from the many experts now offering this. The safeguards to protect investors and the procedures to follow in making a complaint about a financial organisation are also explained.

PRINCIPLES OF SAVING AND INVESTING

The great economist John Maynard Keynes defined saving as the excess of income over consumption. Savings grow by adding to an original sum of money or by keeping it in an account which earns interest. If you take out the interest, you will have left only the money with which you started. This is 'safe' saving without 'growth'. Meanwhile prices rise, and the amount saved buys a smaller amount of goods or services each year. If prices rise by 7 per cent, £10,000 becomes worth only £7,130 after five years, and will be halved (£5,083) in ten.

Some people are concerned more with safety than with the growth of their savings, and money on deposit in UK banks or building societies is safe. It just does not grow in line with prices. On the other hand, such deposit money can be withdrawn immediately, or at short notice if you need it.

Investing is trickier than saving...and riskier. It means backing an enterprise with your cash so that you can eventually share in its success. You hope that your income will rise through growing dividends and that the value of your holding (the price you originally paid to invest) will go up. However, the firm might go broke, so that you would end up with nothing but regrets.

Some of your investments should always be liquid – that is, in cash or a form that can easily be turned into cash without loss. How much depends on what you have to spare and how quickly you may need it in an emergency. There are compensation schemes which guarantee protection for part of your savings and investments, and these are described under 'Protection for Investors'. However, none fully covers larger amounts (over £50,000) so remember: *Caveat Emptor* (Buyer Beware).

Risk is involved in investment because nobody can guarantee the results, which may vary from year to year. The value of your assets can fall as well as rise. So can prices on the Stock

Exchange or other markets because of changes in interest and exchange rates or events at home and abroad, about which you and many other people know nothing.

How do you build up a good portfolio that is a mix of different savings and investment schemes? What principles can help you get the best value from your money?

A portfolio must suit your particular circumstances and indeed your personality. Analyse your objectives. Are you looking for growth...or income, or both? How much are you prepared to risk....if anything? What is your tax position? Are you single: with or without dependants? What are your current assets and existing commitments? How old...and healthy... are you? Are you averse to certain kinds of investment on ethical or sentimental grounds?

Having answered these questions, you can then go on to consider the main requirements of any portfolio. They are liquidity, risk and reward. The last two elements go together: the greater the risk, the greater usually is the chance of reward...or loss. In addition, there is flexibility: never putting all your eggs in one basket and always having some funds which you can get at quickly in case of need.

Another element is your tax position, for some investment schemes are more beneficial taxwise and offer a greater net reward (or Capital Gains Tax advantage) than others. In addition, timing affects the return on your investments, particularly when buying or selling shares or gilt edged securities. In the future too you may not want, or be less able, to cope with the paperwork and complications of investments, even though these may not seem problems now.

In the following pages, various kinds of savings and investments options are discussed in detail. Some 'model' portfolios, which might suit your particular circumstances, are also outlined on pages 94–96.

On page 50 there is a cautionary Checklist to look at before deciding on a particular financial scheme or parting with any money.

Checklist

Risk and Protection Is the value of the capital guaranteed? How much of your investment will be covered by a protection scheme? Are you dealing with a 'tied' agent who can sell you the products of only one company, or an independent adviser who can suggest options from the whole market (see also pp 54–55)? You must be given 'a buyer's guide' to explain the difference.

Is the adviser paid by fee (often the case with solicitors and accountants) or by commission (usually the case with tied sales people)? To what self-regulatory body do they belong?

Liquidity For how long will your money be tied up? Are your circumstances likely to change during this time? How long is the notice period, if any, before you can cash in your investment or part of it? Is there a penalty charged for early withdrawal? When is interest (or a dividend) paid?

Growth Do you need a regular income, or can you afford to wait for a rising one? What are the minimum and maximum sums required for investing? Does the investment offer growth prospects?

Effect on tax How will Independent Taxation and the abolition of composite rate tax affect your income? How will future changes (part time-work, etc) affect your tax position? Is interest (or a dividend) paid gross, or is tax deducted at source?

Long-term prospects Are you sacrificing essentials to benefit your heirs? What would happen to the investment if you should die before realising the proceeds?

PAYING LESS TAX

As Einstein stated 'The hardest thing in the world to understand is income tax.' Whether you agree or not, when deciding about your savings and investments, aim for maximum tax avoidance. Evading tax due is against the law, but arranging your financial affairs so as to attract the least possible tax should be considered by everyone.

As from April 1990, tax avoidance has been part of the new system of Independent Taxation (explained on page 13). In 1991 two further changes have made avoidance easier both for taxpayers and those not liable for tax. Since January, even if you pay tax at the higher rate, you can now invest a total of £9,000 (spread over five years) in a Tax Exempt Special Savings Account (TESSA) offered by banks and building societies, as explained on pages 66–67.

Since 6 April if you are a non-taxpayer, you have been able to avoid paying tax on interest earned from a bank or building society account. You must apply for exemption by filling in form R85, (obtainable from building societies, banks, post offices and tax offices) and will then get interest paid gross on your accounts. If you do not apply for exemption, tax will be deducted at the basic rate and you will have to reclaim it by sending in a certificate of tax paid at the end of the financial year (see also page 37).

However, most National Savings accounts automatically pay interest without deduction of tax and will continue to do this, so there is no need to fill in a form for these accounts.

Tax avoidance should also be considered by people retiring to other countries. If you are planning to live permanently abroad, you could put your savings in an offshore account such as those operating in the Channel Islands or Isle of Man. For safety choose one of the subsidiaries of a major bank or building society. Note also that if you (or your wife) have a home in the UK as well as abroad, this could affect your 'domicile' and make you liable for tax on any income earned in this country.

Wherever you place your savings, interest earned (other than on certain National Savings products) must be entered on your tax return. Whether you are liable for tax or not, if you earn interest of £500 or more each year, your bank must notify the Inland Revenue, while building societies have to report interest paid of more than £1,400; and the Inland Revenue can demand details of smaller amounts. As explained on pages 20–21, once your income reaches a certain level, you start losing the Personal Allowance and the Married Couple's Allowance.

For further information, read the free leaflet *Can you stop paying tax on your bank and building society interest?* (IR 110)

USING PLASTIC CARDS

Use plastic cards only as a way of making money work for you, not as a route to debt. Credit cards allow you to postpone for a short while the payment of goods you have purchased. Debit cards are a form of electronic cheque. They take funds immediately from your current account and, like the charge cards issued by the larger stores, allow you to get overdrawn (but at a high cost).

If cards help you borrow more cheaply because of the interest-free time lapse between 'buying' the goods, and paying for them several weeks later, then – and only then – are they worth while. Lloyds and Barclays make annual charges of £12.00 and £8.00 respectively on their credit cards. Since April, Midland has exacted a £5.00 charge for its Access card holders who want to settle with post-dated cheques. The other banks are 'reviewing' the situation and may also impose charges in the future.

Charge cards issued by department stores, garage chains, etc give you credit on purchases at usually very high interest rates. If you can stand the discipline, it makes better sense to save in a deposit account, withdraw your money when you see goods you want to buy, and thereby get a discount by buying with cash.

Money from a cash dispenser requires a cash or service card. Some of these cards, like Connect and Switch, also work as debit cards, allowing you to buy goods over the counter with the money being debited from your current account. This seems simpler and safer than carrying cash around, but there is always the risk of fraud or loss. To minimise these dangers, *never* write down your personal identity number.

It sometimes makes sense to have a couple of bank or building society cards, even for accounts where you keep small sums. You can use the accounts for different purposes: for writing cheques, using a cash dispenser, getting high interest for money on deposit, buying goods on credit.

GETTING FINANCIAL ADVICE

Advice on money matters can come from many different experts. They include accountants, bank managers, insurance sales people, solicitors, stockbrokers and actuaries. A new trend in recent years has been the opening of firms calling themselves money shops or financial consultants. In some cases these are simply insurance and mortgage brokers operating under a new name. Others aim to give an all-round service, especially to retired people, from a variety of experts such as former bankers or accountants. The Securities and Investments Board (SIB) has a central registry detailing what kind of business a financial adviser is authorised to do, and you can contact the board at the address on page 117.

Unless these advisers quote a fee, their remuneration will be a commission from whatever plans they recommend – be it unit trusts, managed bonds or life insurance. The Financial Services Act outlaws unauthorised salespeople who offer to take your money for investment. The Act also makes it illegal for an agent to give biased advice unless the agent shows that he/she is 'tied' to, or employed by, the company recommended. With very few exceptions most building societies and banks are tied to the products they offer.

Despite these safeguards, there are continual reports of pressurised selling and unsuitable investments being offered, often with older people as victims. Sometimes salespeople may even have been given information about potential buyers by a bank or building society. Be on your guard against 'sharp practice'.

The difficulty in getting the correct advice for your personal circumstances amid the constant changes in the financial world has led to the formation of the Money Management Council, which operates as an educational resource centre (address on page 116). Its reports are circulated by Citizens Advice Bureaux, and they can also be obtained by writing to the Council, enclosing an SAE.

Before seeking advice from a financial consultant or buying any product from a broker, you should keep the following points in mind:

- First, make sure the company or individual giving advice belongs to a professional organisation (see also pp 56–57).
- Secondly, find out from friends about reputable sources of financial advice, or ask the nearest Citizens Advice Bureau, which has several hundred 'points of contact' throughout the UK. The Bureaux include some representatives who will visit people in hospital or in other institutions who need information and advice. This service is in addition to CAB permanent offices in the UK, backed up by Money Advice Support Units which in 1991 operate in 18 towns including London, Belfast, Halifax, Liverpool. Manchester, Oxford, and Wolverhampton. They provide a special service for people with credit problems.
- Thirdly, be prepared to discuss all circumstances which might have a bearing on how your money should be invested.
- Fourthly, if you approach a new financial adviser, be wary about being encouraged to cash in everything and start again. Commission based salespeople are not going to earn any money by telling you to keep what you've got. Negotiate an upfront fee and a rebate of commission on any new investments. You should also avoid recommendations for frequent switching of your money from one fund to another.
- Finally, keep up to date by reading the financial sections of newspapers and magazines and following the money programmes on television and radio (see p 119). Another source of information is an exhibition like the Money Show, usually held annually in various cities in the UK. In 1991, it took place in the Barbican, London, with 50 seminars and over 100 financial companies exhibiting. These included banks, building societies, unit trusts, financial advisers and National Savings, as well as newspaper, radio and TV money specialists, all of whom are available for personal enquiries.

PROTECTION FOR INVESTORS

The Financial Services Act 1986 – in force since April 1988 –
has not yet achieved all that was hoped for in terms of investor
protection or compensation. What it has done is to establish a
comprehensive regulatory framework, and every effort has
been made to detect fraud or misconduct. However, there are,
and always will be, fools and knaves in financial institutions
as elsewhere. If someone is determined to defraud investors,
they usually succeed, so, to repeat, the rule must still be
Caveat Emptor (buyer beware).

Some types of investment are not covered by the Act. They
include bank and building society accounts, mortgages or
loans, investments in property, stamps, precious stones,
antiques, cars or other 'tangible' goods.

The Act is implemented by a network of watchdog
organisations headed by the Securities and Investments Board
(SIB) whose address is listed on page 117. Other watchdogs
are the Self Regulatory Organisations (SROs) and the
Recognised Professional Bodies (RPBs). Any company or firm
carrying on investment business in the UK must be authorised
by one of these SROs or RPBs. To check whether your
financial adviser or a particular company is authorised, ring
SIB's Central Register (071–929 36520).

Self Regulatory Organisations (SROs)

The Financial Services Act requires that financial
organisations (even independent consultants) belong to one of
the following SROs: the Financial Intermediaries, Managers &
Brokers Regulatory Association (FIMBRA); the Life Assurance
& Unit Trust Regulatory Organisation (LAUTRO); the
Investors Management Regulatory Organisation (IMRO); and
the Securities and Futures Authority (SFA). The addresses of
these organisations are on pages 115-117.

Recognised Professional Bodies (RPBs)

Solicitors, accountants and actuaries whose main activity is not in investment get authorisation to give financial advice from their own recognised professional bodies (RPBs). These 9 RPBs comprise the Law Societies of England and Wales, Scotland and Northern Ireland (3), the Institute of Chartered and Certified Accountants in England and Wales, Scotland and Ireland (4), the Insurance Brokers' Registration Council and the Institute of Actuaries (2).

How to complain

If you have grounds – such as dishonesty, negligence or incompetence – to be dissatisfied with an organisation, take up the matter first with the head of the firm. If your complaint is not resolved satisfactorily, you should apply to the appropriate RPB or SRO (listed on the stationery of authorised businesses), which will explain how you should proceed in making a formal complaint. If the SRO cannot deal with the complaint, they may refer you to the relevant ombudsman. Finally, if you still feel that the RPB or SRO has not dealt with the situation properly, write to the Securities and Investments Board.

This procedure for making a complaint is free, but there is always the option to withdraw the case and take legal action against the organisation (at your own expense) unless and until you accept a monetary settlement in full and final settlement of your claim or agree to abide by a binding adjudication/arbitration procedure.

How to get compensation

The Securities and Investments Board has also set up an Investors' Compensation Scheme (ICS) which pays out when investors lose money through the collapse of an authorised firm, provided that the firm is declared in default by ICS and the relevant criteria for dissatisfaction are met. However, companies with only interim authorisation are not covered under the scheme. The maximum amount of compensation is 100 per cent of the first £30,000 invested and 90 per cent of the next £20,000, which means that the limit of compensation will normally be £48,000 to each investor.

To appeal for compensation from an organisation which belongs to IMRO, you should get in touch with the Office of Investment Referee (address on page 117). However, do note that compensation only covers investments made since 29 April 1988, and that the limit is £100,000 except for special agreements.

Investors in an authorised insurance company which collapses are protected under the Policy Holders Protection Act. This pays up to 90 per cent of the investment with no maximum limit – for example, if you had a 20-year endowment policy but after 10 years the company collapsed, you would be entitled to 90 per cent of the 10-year value of the policy, as determined by an actuary.

Experience since the end of the Second World War shows that on the few occasions when a building society has been in difficulties, it has been taken over by another, to protect depositors. However, in the unlikely event of a building society collapsing, compensation from the Building Societies Association is limited to 90 per cent of the first £20,000, that is, £18,000.

The large banks used to have a generous compensation scheme because it was considered unlikely ever to be needed. Now the guaranteed compensation has dwindled to a mere 75 per cent of £20,000 or £15,000. If safety is your over riding consideration, it makes sense (though not money), to split up your savings between a couple of banks and building societies even though interest is usually much higher on large sums deposited.

The Law Society's indemnity fund covers claims for negligence against its members (including solicitors who recommend investments) up to £1 million. In cases of dishonesty, it can also make unlimited compensation payments. Since the passage of the Courts and Legal Services Act 1990, the Solicitors Complaints Bureau is allowed to award compensation up to £1,000 to anyone who has suffered 'inadequate professional service' from a solicitor (address on page 117).

Members of the Institute of Chartered Accountants must take out indemnity insurance related to the size of their business, with a minimum of £50,000. If they hold more than £50,000 of clients' money, they must have additional insurance to cover that amount, and take 'reasonable steps' to ensure that they are able to meet any claims against them. Some firms of investment advisers also carry heavy insurance against the possibility of loss by a client through negligence or dishonesty.

Do be aware that the Investors Compensation Scheme makes a distinction between awarding money and paying compensation, so that the whole process is still very complicated for the ordinary person. Take care, especially when considering investing in offshore funds or collective investment schemes from abroad (including the European Community). These can be sold in Britain if the SIB is confident that local supervision is as strict as that which exists here. Currently offshore funds offer no protection to the investor, who should therefore only invest in offshore subsidiaries of well-known banks or building societies.

Ombudsmen

Three separate arbitrators or ombudsmen specialise in complaints about banks; building societies; insurance companies and unit trusts. In addition there are three recently appointed Ombudsmen: one for Legal Services (appointed under the Courts and Legal Services Act 1990) to oversee the handling of complaints against solicitors, barristers and licensed conveyancers. The Office of the Ombudsman for Corporate Estate Agents deals with complaints against corporate estate agencies whose members join voluntarily but must then abide by a Code of Practice.

The Office of the Pensions Ombudsman began work in April 1991 in association with the Occupational Pensions Advisory Service (OPAS) for complaints and enquiries about personal and company pension schemes. OPAS can be contacted through local Citizen's Advice Bureaux, or at the address on page 116.

It is perhaps worth noting that except for the Pensions Ombudsman, all the others are funded by their member organisations. Ombudsmen can rule on a variety of grievances involving dishonesty, incompetence, negligence and inconvenience, and can order compensation for varying levels: up to £100,000 maximum except for permanent health insurance (£10,000), and up to £50,000 for a complaint against a bank which occurred before 15 January 1988.

Nevertheless, Ombudsmen do not have unlimited powers. The Building Societies Ombudsman is legally empowered to investigate organisations in his sector, whereas some of his counterparts, who act for other industries, operate under voluntary schemes. For instance, the Banking Ombudsman's rulings are accepted by most banks which handle private accounts. Most complaints tend to be about automatic cash dispensers, which are also a source of grievance for the Building Societies Ombudsman.

Since January 1991, the Unit Trust Ombudsman has been realigned with the Insurance Ombudsman, but not all insurance companies recognise the rulings of the Ombudsman.

The procedure for appealing to an Ombudsman is the same as that for an SRO, as explained on page 57. The addresses for the Ombudsmen discussed in the section above are on pages 114-118. It does not matter if you do not know which Ombudsman to approach first, as they work closely together and will redirect complaints to the relevant office. The procedure is free, and you can withdraw your complaint at any stage. Many cases are settled early on, although final rulings may not always favour the complainants.

BUILDING SOCIETY SERVICES/ ACCOUNTS

Building societies used to be simply for saving and investing, as safe as houses (and in some cases, even safer) not least because they were owned mutually by both borrowers and investors. What has changed dramatically in recent years are building societies' services and products. Most societies now offer a range of services from cheque books and consumer credit to insurance and stockbroking.

When a building society changes its activities, you should ensure that these are to the advantage of its members. Changes are not always for the better, as shown in the last few years by the biggest societies which have had problems with new ventures.

There has also been concern expressed about misleading advertising being placed by some societies, which offer home loans at supposedly cheap rates and in foreign currencies. As a result, since February 1990 all advertisements have warned potential customers of the risk involved in foreign currency investments, as international currency rates fluctuate.

In any case, look carefully when considering a mortgage from a lender not a member of the Building Societies Association or outside the jurisdiction of the Building Societies or Banking Ombudsmen. In case of a complaint, you may find it hard to get compensation – without having to pay legal costs – except by appealing through the Office of Fair Trading (address on page 117).

Lending money

The law under which building societies currently operate requires that at least 82.5 per cent of their commercial assets (total assets less fixed and liquid assets) are in loans to individuals for house purchase. These must be secured by a mortgage with no more than 100 per cent of the value of the property being lent at any one time.

Some societies also lend for general purposes where the borrower provides a property as security. In addition, they offer lending facilities of special interest to older people, such as a remortgage whereby a dwindling or paid-off mortgage is exchanged for a new larger one based on the increased value of the property.

If you are a taxpayer and are considering paying off a mortgage with a lump sum (from an insurance policy or a redundancy payment, for example), there are two factors to think about.

First, if you dispense with a loan on which you get mortgage relief at source (through MIRAS), you will get no tax relief on a new loan unless it is for a home income plan or other 'qualifying' purpose. Instead, you will have to pay normal interest charges on that loan, and these could be quite high.

The second factor to consider is the change in interest-rate levels which might mean that you would be able to use the lump sum to better effect, as shown below.

Example
Vic and Marjorie have an outstanding mortgage on their home of £18,000 on which the 14.5 per cent interest is (after 25 per cent MIRAS) payable at 10.875 per cent. If they could invest a lump sum of £18,000 for a higher interest return than 10.875 per cent net – for example, in two TESSAs and a high-interest building society deposit account – they could pay off their monthly mortgage and (depending on interest rates over a five-year period) even have a bit left over as profit. If the deposit interest rates were to go higher, so too would their profit. If rates were to fall, Vic and Marjorie would need to consider retrieving their lump sum to pay off the mortgage.

■ Before going ahead with any changes in or a repayment of your mortgage, always get impartial advice. See also Age Concern England's publication *Using Your Home as Capital*, which has full details about remortgages (price and details for ordering on page 121).

Cards and cheques

Many societies now offer accounts with services such as cash dispensers, standing order facilities, cheque books for free banking and interest (though not at the highest rates). However, charges may be made for a cheque if the balance in the account falls below a certain sum. A few societies also stipulate minimum and maximum sums for certain accounts. Others have no such limits.

Ordinary account

This is a flexible way to invest, as there are few restrictions on how much and how often you may make withdrawals. If you do not need the full services of a bank and write out few cheques, an ordinary (or share) account might be a useful place for ready cash. The minimum investment is £1.00, and there is no maximum.

Interest is paid on a daily basis and credited half-yearly to your account or directly to you.

Cashing in depends on the rules of the particular society. You can take out a certain amount in cash immediately, or ask for a cheque for larger amounts.

■ Note that for non-taxpayers, it is now possible to receive building society and bank account interest free of tax (see page 17 for more details).

Extra-interest account

Different building societies have special names and different terms for this account. It pays top rates of interest, but the minimum lump sum to open the account varies as does the notice period. If you want to withdraw your money immediately, you lose interest for the period of official notice; and if the balance in the account falls below the minimum allowed, your money may be transferred to an ordinary share account.

There is no legal maximum for an extra-interest account, but the ceiling established by individual societies ranges between £100,000 and £2 million.

Interest may be payable monthly, quarterly, half-yearly or annually, or it can be left to accumulate in the account and earn more interest.

The most recent development among extra interest accounts are ones with all transactions being done by post. These often pay the highest interest rates.

Monthly income account

Most building societies now offer accounts with monthly interest paid on lump sums. Depending on the terms of the account, there is usually a penalty for an immediate withdrawal.

Fixed-term account

Higher rates of interest are often offered to investors who promise to keep a lump sum with the society for a fixed period of time – between one and five years. The longer the term, the higher the rate will be. If the ordinary share rate changes during that time, so will the return on your fixed-term account. Usually the smaller and less well-known societies offer the best rates, so ask for details of their contracts. Interest is paid monthly or half-yearly, directly to you, to your bank account or accumulated in the account.

Cashing in varies between societies. With some you cannot cash in before the agreed period expires. The only money you can withdraw is the interest earned. Therefore, it is important not to commit money for a longer term than you can cope with, even if the interest rate looks attractive.

Bank-linked account

A few societies offer an account which can be twinned with a current account at certain banks so that some of your money always earns interest. Though withdrawals are made through your bank account, interest is credited automatically to the building society account at rates similar to those for an ordinary account.

Tax Exempt Special Savings Account
(TESSA)

Known as TESSA for short, this account became available in January 1991 for people aged 18 or over. The rules are simple. You may have one TESSA only and must hold it for five years. The maximum you can invest is a total of £9,000 spread over the five years but with limits of £3,000 in year one and £1,800 in subsequent years. (Regular savings TESSAs are also on offer.) All interest earned is tax free. If withdrawn, it is paid net and the tax element retained in the TESSA until the end of the five-year period. If the capital is touched, the tax exemption goes and the account becomes a normal deposit account.

Are TESSAs worth having? For taxpayers who can afford the five year wait, the answer is yes. Non-taxpayers may be able to find better gross interest elsewhere without locking up their money for five years. The best TESSA to choose is one offered by a bank or building society, paying a high interest rate and a bonus, and without a withdrawal penalty if you switch during the five years to another (better paying) TESSA. But competition for your deposits is likely to remain fierce, and the best rates are likely to remain so.

The TESSA rates are variable. At the time of writing the only five-year fixed one to come on offer was Britannia Building Society (12.25 per cent) which was fully subscribed before the end of January 1991. Save & Prosper has fixed interest for the first year (1991) only at 13 per cent. If other accounts emerge during the summer of 1991, consider the possibility that rates might rise, leaving you with a lower fixed rate.

For more information about TESSAs, you should read the *Good Tessa Guide* (address and details on page 119). Also useful is a free leaflet published by the Building Society Shop (address on page 114); but note that they receive a commission from the societies recommended.

Offshore accounts

Based usually in the Isle of Man, an offshore account offered by several societies pays interest gross without self-certification, though it must be declared on both the instant access and notice accounts. Up to £500 can be withdrawn in cash, larger amounts by cheque (send in your application with a passbook) or by telegraphic transfer. These accounts are useful for people who don't want to bother certifying that they are non-taxpayers and for those working or living abroad.

FRIENDLY SOCIETY PLANS

These began two centuries ago partly as burial clubs. They are still useful for saving up funeral money or a small sum for any other purpose. Some, like the Manchester Unity Society, stress the social aspects of membership; others, the importance of health insurance. Of the 400 societies still operating, only about a hundred do any new business, and 85 per cent of the friendly societies' growth is produced by eight of them.

Members must usually be between 18 and 70 years of age, but Odd Fellows of Manchester offers assurance to 85 at next birthday. Friendly society plans are tax exempt and provide a fixed amount of £1,125 as life assurance for savers who join a plan before the age of 55. After this the cover reduces by £30.00 every year, so that for somebody aged 60 years, for example, the life cover would be £925. Ultimately only what you have saved (plus interest) will be returned on death. You can invest up to £13.50 monthly, £150 annually, or £1,175 as a lump sum.

New rules under the 1991 Budget will allow up to £18.00 monthly, £200 yearly in regular savings for children in ten-year tax exempt friendly society schemes, though there could be penalties for early surrender of one of these.

Look closely at the management expenses of friendly society plans, as these become relatively heavy, owing to the small size of the societies. The amount deducted for life assurance should be clearly stated. Check also that the quoted rate of return is as good as the best return offered by building societies. For checking on the credentials of a plan, you should refer to the Registrar of Friendly Societies at the address on page 117.

■ Note that forthcoming Government regulations will widen the powers of the societies so that they can offer a range of financial services. It will also enhance the powers of the regulators.

BANK/FINANCE COMPANY ACCOUNTS

In addition to the four major clearing banks, there are many other banks in existence, including the Co-op, Girobank, the TSB and Abbey National. Under the Banking Act of 1987, the Bank of England, through its Board of Supervision, oversees these various banks and other deposit takers. Known as 'authorised institutions', all of these have to conform to certain criteria, such as adequate capital and reserves, accounting and other record keeping procedures.

An authorised institution can call itself a 'bank' if it has at least £5 million of share capital. The Deposit Protection Scheme covers deposits to a maximum of only £15,000 (75 per cent of £20,000), and the Banking Ombudsman deals with complaints involving maladministration but not about commercial decisions on loans. So if you cannot get a loan from a bank at the rate you require, you should try another bank, but above all, avoid loan 'sharks'.

Most banks offer a variety of accounts, including high-interest ones, depending on the amount and time lapse before withdrawal. A useful service for retired people is the transfer of pensions, dividends and interest into an account. Another facility is an account which you can operate from home seven days a week, 18 hours a day, through a telephone linked to a screen. The necessary equipment can be purchased for around £100, in addition to a monthly subscription of £3.00; and these charges are waived by the Bank of Scotland if you maintain a balance of £500 in your current account.

Bank opening hours are now more flexible. Main Co-op branches stay open until 5 pm on weekdays; and the Handybanks within the Co-op stores are open on Saturdays, as are many of the big bank branches until noon. Most Abbey National branches (all of which now function as banks) also work on Saturday mornings, except those in the City.

Although loyalty to one bank over many years ought to stand you in good stead with the manager, this is not guaranteed when you face temporary difficulties or need a special favour. It pays to shop around for the different services outlined below.

Current account

The major banks are phasing out traditional current accounts in favour of those which pay interest on credit balances, though do note that you may have to apply for this. Charges are made when the account is overdrawn. This so-called free banking, meaning no charges when there is a favourable balance, usually penalises depositors who go into the red.

The fact that some banks have several new types of current account makes a straightforward comparison between their rates almost impossible. The best course is to consider what you want from a current account (good accounting, transfer systems, a standing order facility, automatic cash dispensers, cheque book, credit cards, etc) and keep the minimum for these purposes in that account. In order to avoid charges and to earn more interest, put the bulk of your savings elsewhere.

CHARGES FOR CURRENT ACCOUNTS

Current account charges may alter suddenly when interest rates change. Arranged borrowing is cheaper than borrowing money from the bank without warning, so it is wise to consult with the bank manager when you foresee being short of money for a certain period of time. As an example, Girobank charges 1.9 per cent monthly for authorised, 2.5 per cent for unauthorised overdrafts.

The Royal Bank of Scotland charges £2.00 per quarter for overdrawn current accounts, with or without formal agreement, the Bank of Scotland a maintenance charge of £3.50 if the balance falls below an average of £550. This average balance is usually the minimum required for free banking by the other major banks (Natwest, Lloyds, Barclays, Midland, TSB). More is usually necessary to earn the highest rates. Natwest makes no charge on current account overdrafts if the average balance in the charging period is £500, but you have to pay £30.00 quarterly for unauthorised borrowing and £15.00 for an overdraft letter.

Deposit account

This account is no longer such good value as it used to be. Unless the deposit is for £50,000 or more, or you have applied to have interest paid net, tax will be taken off the interest before you get it. Non-taxpayers are likely to be better off putting their money elsewhere.

However, there are often valid reasons for leaving funds on deposit, and most banks will undertake to keep your current account automatically topped up from your deposit account. This can save you bank charges if your current account falls below the stipulated limit. The minimum investment is £1.00.

Interest is calculated daily and credited to the account at certain fixed intervals, usually half yearly. Rates rise and fall in line with current rates in the money market; but whatever happens to the rate, you cannot lose your original deposit. Generally, the return from most banks does not match the highest rates paid by building societies. To keep the full amount of interest earned, you must give notice for withdrawing all or part of your account.

High-interest cheque account (HICA)

These accounts may have special names (Barclays Prime Account, Benchmark Premier, Royal Bank of Scotland Premier, etc) as well as or instead of HICA; but all of them pay higher interest than that earned in an ordinary deposit account. If the balance in your account slips below the minimum investment figure, the interest paid to you may fall quite sharply. It is usually added to the capital, with basic-rate tax deducted at source. High-interest accounts also provide a cheque book with, usually, a limit to the minimum amount that can be written – for example, £100.

The interest on HICAs reflects what is happening in the City's money markets, where money from high-interest accounts is being invested. The higher the deposit balance, usually the higher the interest offered. But this is not the case with all HICAs. Where interest is added on yearly, the compound annual rate will be lower than that for the same interest added on monthly or quarterly.

Gross, net and compound annual rates (CAR) and details on how often interest is added (monthly, quarterly, annually) are given in the *Financial Times* under the heading Money Market Funds.

HICAs are offered by finance companies, merchant banks and fund managers as well as the large banks. Study the small print about the amount which can be withdrawn and the notice period required for withdrawals or even for closing the account.

Monthly income account

The money you invest earns interest which is paid directly into your current account each month. You decide how much income you want each month and invest enough to produce this. For up-to-date information about these accounts, Money Guides (address on page 119) produce a monthly list of what they consider the best value offered by banks, building societies and others, as well as the minimum deposit and period of notice required.

Fixed-term deposit account

You invest a lump sum for a specified time. Interest is paid at agreed periods during the term, and the lump sum is repaid when the term is up. As your only chance to withdraw your capital comes at the end of the fixed term, it is important not to tie up money you are likely to need quickly in this kind of account. The minimum investment is between £1,500 and £5,000.

In the case of the death of the investor or of extreme hardship, the bank will release the money before the end of the investment term; but the interest may be reduced.

Where a deposit was made in a fixed-term account before 6 July 1984, interest continues to be paid gross. Therefore it is not necessary for non-taxpayers to apply for exemption from tax.

Other accounts

Since January 1991 banks have been offering Save As You Earn (SAYE) accounts, in addition to Tax Exempt Special Savings Accounts (TESSAs) which operate under the same rules as those applying to building societies (see also p 65).

Finance company accounts

DEPOSIT ACCOUNT

Finance company deposit accounts are similar to those offered by the major banks, but the companies pay higher interest for usually a higher degree of customer risk. You deposit your money for either an agreed period of time or on condition that you will give a certain period of notice before withdrawing – say, three or six months. Interest net of basic tax is paid out every three or six months or accumulated, depending on the company, so you should check these details with them before investing.

Look at finance company advertisements and study their brochures thoroughly. For authorised institutions, the compensation scheme is the same as that applying to the banks – namely, 75 per cent of up to £20,000 invested is guaranteed safe, whatever happens to the company.

MONEY FUND

This account requires a large lump sum which you can get back very quickly or at short notice. At the same time, the rate of interest is favourable because the money is invested in the money market where the interest rates are high. The minimum investment may be between £1,000 and £2,500.

The *Financial Times* lists the daily (variable) rate of interest paid by different Money Market Funds. On most accounts, it is paid half-yearly by cheque or added to the account quarterly, depending on the fund.

Girobank accounts

The big difference between Girobank and other bank current accounts is that cash can be withdrawn at post offices. The Keyway account, which is interest bearing, with a £100 cheque guarantee card, is particularly useful for withdrawals of up to £100 at any post office. People with a current account may also open one of the high interest savings accounts (Blue Chip). The charity account (minimum £500) offers a good rate of interest to the depositor and pays 1 per cent of your balance to one of several charities you may nominate, including Age Concern. Leaflets about other Girobank services are available at post offices.

NATIONAL SAVINGS

National Savings should not be ignored when deciding where to put your money for a safe return. Although their competitive edge has now been blunted because bank and building society accounts pay tax gross to non-taxpayers, various National Savings products can still prove very useful to savers. In addition to those outlined on the following pages, there are Gilts (as Government stocks are called) on the National Savings Stock Register, explained on p 80.

Also worth noting is the fact that National Savings products bought for children by grandparents are regarded as the child's own income and are therefore tax free to the limit of the Personal Allowance. If bought by parents for a child, interest of more than £100, from 6 April 1991, is treated as the parent's own income for tax purposes. A Children's Bonus Bond (on sale from July 1991) for those under 16 pays a large bonus after five years and could make suitable presents for grandchildren.

Investments and Accounts

CAPITAL BOND (SERIES C)

This is for people who want a compound interest rate return on their investment over five years of 11.5 per cent, gross. A statement of value is sent each year. There is no exemption form for non-taxpayers to fill in. However, no interest is paid on any amount if the bond is encashed before the first anniversary of purchase. The bonds may be bought in multiples of £100; and the maximum total holding in all Series of Capital Bonds, excluding any holding of Series A, is £100,000.

Growth in value of Series C Bond

Growth added at end of year	£100 bond	£5,000 bond	Percentage Increase
Year 1	£7.00	£350.00	7.00
Year 2	£9.36	£468.13	8.75
Year 3	£12.80	£639.99	11.00
Year 4	£17.76	£887.99	13.75
Year 5	£25.42	£1,270.88	17.30
Repayment Value	£172.34	£8,616.99	11.5%

INCOME BOND

This provides a monthly income with interest paid gross. The current rate, which can change, is 13 per cent paid on the 5th of each month. The minimum purchase is £5,000, and the maximum holding for investments made since December 1989 is £25,000. The interest rate may be varied at six weeks' notice and interest can be credited to your bank, building society or National Savings Investment Account. Withdrawals (in £1,000 multiples) are paid by a crossed warrant. They require three months' notice, and interest at only half the published rate is repaid for those made in the first year.

ORDINARY ACCOUNT

The advantages of this account are the convenience for some people of banking at a post office and that the first £70.00 of interest is tax free. The account pays only 2½ per cent standard rate and a higher rate of 5 per cent on a balance of £500 or more held for a complete calendar year. This is credited annually on 31 December. The minimum investment is £5.00 and the maximum is £10,000. If you withdraw over £50.00 on demand (the maximum is £100), your bank book will be kept for checking. For larger amounts you have to fill in an application form and send it with your book to the National Savings Bank, Glasgow. Payment will be authorised in a few days.

Anybody with an account in one post office for at least six months, can apply for a Regular Customer Account. This allows immediate daily withdrawals of up to £250 in cash on demand at that particular post office without the book being held back. It can be used in the normal way at any other post office.

INVESTMENT ACCOUNT

This account is mainly for non-taxpayers, as the interest (currently 12.25 per cent but variable) is paid gross and credited automatically each year on December 31. For all withdrawals – even if you want to take out only the interest – you must give one month's notice (starting from the day your postal application is received at National Savings headquarters). The minimum for each deposit made is £5.00; the maximum holding is £25,000 except for those made before 31 December 1989, which may remain invested.

PREMIUM BOND

This has more to do with gambling than saving money, although you can always get back just as much as you put in. The minimum investment for someone over the age of 16 is £100, but if you are buying a bond for a child younger than 16, the minimum is £10.00. The maximum holding is £10,000, in units of £10.00.

No interest is paid on the bond; but after holding one for three whole calendar months, you become eligible for the monthly prize draw with the chance of winning one of over 200,000 prizes ranging from £50.00 to £250,000. Premium Bonds are ideal only for gamblers because you lose nothing except for what might be gained by putting money elsewhere, and there is a far likelier chance than in most gambling ventures of winning something.

■ **Commit only a tiny amount of money, just for the fun of it, to a Premium Bond.**

Certificates

OLD ISSUES

With certificates, National Savings supersede one issue with another at short notice. When interest rates seem to be at their highest, it is a good idea to buy the latest issue before it is replaced by another, likely to pay less. Certain issues, no longer on sale, may be kept indefinitely; but it is not always wise to do this, as there are often better investments elsewhere.

Certificates usually have an issue life of five years. After that the interest is paid for the 7th to the 31st fixed interest issues at a common rate called the General Extension Rate at 5.01 per cent. Early issues have very low interest rates, so review your certificates annually rather than hold on to them, as you may get a better rate by cashing them in and reinvesting.

YEARLY PLAN

This is a regular saving scheme enabling you to buy a Yearly Plan Certificate with a guaranteed interest rate. It requires a standing order over a year of £20.00 a month (minimum) up to £200 (maximum) in multiples of £5.00. The interest rate is added on to the capital sum and itself earns interest.

To get this maximum return, equivalent to 8.5 per cent compounded annually, 12 payments must be made and the certificate held for a further four years. The tax-free interest is paid when the certificates are cashed in. There is an Extension Rate for certificates after the fourth anniversary of issue if at least seven payments have been made. You may start a fresh Yearly Plan every 12 months. Early withdrawals are allowed, but if they are made in the first year, no interest is paid. The normal notice period is two weeks.

See also the leaflet *What are Your Certificates Earning?* DNS/555/9001, available from Freephone 0800–868 700 and from post offices.

36TH ISSUE

The 36th issue certificates, available in units of £25.00, pay 8.5 per cent interest compounded annually if held for at least five years. Earlier encashment gives a lower rate of return. Interest is earned for each completed period of three months, but nothing is earned on certificates repaid in the first year except on 'reinvestment certificates', meaning the conversion of earlier issues held for at least five years. Such reinvested certificates may also include index-linked ones and inherited ones, providing they are at least five years old.

The maximum holding of 36th issue certificates is £5,000, but you may reinvest from mature savings certificates and Yearly Plan certificates up to a total of £10,000 in addition to the normal limit of £5,000. Each year the certificates are held, they grow in value, as shown below.

Growth in value after five-year period

Purchase price	Value at 8.5%	Growth
£25.00	£37.59	£12.59
£100.00	£150.37	£50.37
£1,000.00	£1,503.66	£503.66
£5,000.00	£7,518.28	£2,518.28

Payment if you cash in early

Minimum period held	Tax-free interest rate
1 Year	5.5% from date of purchase
2 Years	6.0% from date of purchase
3 Years	6.75% from date of purchase
4 Years	7.5% from date of purchase

INDEX-LINKED 5TH ISSUE

Once your money has been invested in this certificate (units of £25.00 only) for at least a year, its value increases in line with the Retail Price Index (RPI), the official measure of how prices are rising. In addition, there is annual interest which works out at 4.5 per cent compounded during the full five years. The maximum holding is £10,000 per person; the reinvestment holding limit is also £10,000.

Certificates can be cashed in at any time, but within the first year you get your money back with no gain. After the first year, certificates benefit from an increase in value in line with rising prices plus additional interest, as shown in the table below. You earn both the index linking and any extra interest monthly from the date of purchase – so if you buy on the 12th of the month, the value of your savings will change on the 12th of each following month.

Growth in value from date of purchase

Period held	Tax-free return
1 year	RPI only
2 years	RPI + 0.5%
3 years	RPI + 1%
4 years	RPI + 2%
5 years	RPI + 4.5%

PUBLIC LOANS

Government stocks (gilts)

Loans to the Government – known as 'gilts' for short – work like this: in return for your money, you get a certificate stating the name of the stock, the date of repayment, if any, and the gross (pre-tax) rate of interest.

Gilts are divided into five categories:

o those coming up for repayment within five years are known as short-dated;

o those with up to fifteen years to run: medium-dated;

o those with a longer life: long-dated;

o those with no time limit for repayment: undated or irredeemables;

o those related to the Retail Price Index: index-linked.

They have different rates of interest. The interest is known as the coupon: 2½ per cent interest is a low coupon, 14 per cent, a high coupon. Interest on all Government stocks is paid half-yearly, except for Consols, on which it is paid quarterly.

You can buy (and sell) gilts through a broker or by post from the Bonds & Stock Office (address on page 116). Application forms and a prepaid envelope for stock on the National Savings Stock Register are available at post offices (grey form GS.1 for buying or the pink one GS.3 for selling).

The maximum amount that may be invested in any one stock in any one day through the Stock Office is £10,000, but there is no limit to the total amount you may hold. Gilts bought through the office pay interest gross, and this must be declared on your tax return.

NOMINAL AND FACE VALUE OF STOCK

The face value of stock is known as its nominal or par value. For every £100 nominal stock you buy, the Government promises to pay back £100 at the maturity (redemption) date. This date is at the end of the title of the stock: for instance, the maturity date of Treasury 13¼ per cent 1993 is 1993, and means that in 1993 you will receive £100 for every £100 of nominal stock you bought.

You can gain or lose on this transaction. Even though the interest is fixed, in this case at 13¼ per cent, the price of the stock moves up or down with the demand for it. As a result, the actual percentage interest you get on your money (its running yield) depends on the price you paid for the stock.

Running yield (gross)

The running yield is calculated by multiplying the nominal price times the coupon and dividing by the market (or purchase) price, as shown below.

(Note that the purchase prices are greatly exaggerated to illustrate the principle.)

Nominal price of stock	Coupon	Purchase price of stock	Amount received per year	Yield
£100	12%	£100	£12	12%
£100	12%	£200	£12	6%
£100	12%	£50	£12	24%

Calculations

12 x 100/100 = 12%
12 x 100/200 = 6%
12 x 100/ 50 = 24%

If you hold on to a stock until redemption, and you paid more than £100 for it, then you will make a loss on your capital, even though you may have gained high interest throughout the life of the stock.

Redemption yield (gross)

In addition to the running yield of a stock, there is a redemption yield. The rough method for calculating this, as shown below, is to add or deduct the difference between the stock's purchase price and its selling or redemption price, and divide that gain or loss by the number of years the stock has been held.

(Note that these are only rough calculations. In practice yields are calculated on formulae which give more accurate answers than the rough approximations shown below.)

Redemption yield (gain)

£100 stock @ 10% (running yield) is sold after 10 years @ £110. Capital gain over 10 years is £10, that is 10% or +1% per year.
Redemption yield = running yield of 10% + 1% = 11%.
(Note that the average gain of 1% per year is added to the running yield.)

Redemption yield (loss)

£100 stock @ 10% (running yield) is sold after 10 years @ £90. Capital loss over 10 years is £10, that is 10% or − 1% per year.
Redemption yield = running yield of 10% − 1% = 9%.
(Note that the average loss of 1% a year is subtracted from the running yield.)

FACTORS TO CONSIDER

When buying gilts, consider whether you prefer high yielding stock or the chance of capital gain – which on gilts is tax free. (But remember that you cannot offset losses against gains elsewhere.)

The commission you pay on small transactions of stock is much less when you deal with the Bonds & Stocks Office rather than buying through a broker: £1.00 for buying or selling up to £250 of stock, 50p for each extra £125 traded. The disadvantage of using the post is the delay in dealing and the fact that you do not know the trading price, as you would when dealing through a broker.

The prices of gilts are affected by interest rates, inflation, the balance of payments and the strength of the pound. So you have the chance to 'buy low' for a tax-free capital gain, with the risk of loss if you have to sell the stock at the wrong time.

Gilts, in their role as 'National Savings' are used to fund the State, which guarantees their security. High taxpayers are normally better off with a low coupon stock bought at a discount. In this way they sacrifice income for a capital gain when the stock matures. But the old practice of buying stocks ex-dividend (XD) and selling them almost six months later (when the price had risen in expectation of the next dividend) has now been stopped.

Corporation stocks

Corporation stock is the general name given to loans raised on the stockmarket by local authorities. This source of funding is now virtually closed, although a few stocks are still quoted on the Stock Exchange. They work in the same way as gilts, except that they are not available through the post office and are not guaranteed by the Government.

Town hall bonds

Local authorities used to raise money by advertising for deposits through the post or over the counter, with fixed interest paid for a known period. As with corporation stocks, this type of funding is now almost extinct. Very few local authorities raise money in this way. For current information, write or phone them directly.

STOCK EXCHANGE INVESTMENTS

Shares

When you buy shares, you are buying a stake in a company which issues them in order to raise capital. Shares are bought and sold on the Stock Exchange, and their prices can fluctuate from day to day. As a shareholder you get part of the profits as a dividend, or if you need ready cash or lose faith in the management, you can sell the shares.

A broker would be unlikely to manage a portfolio of shares worth less than £25,000. The cost of investing involves the broker's commission which is charged whether you buy through a stockbroker or a bank. Furthermore, stamp duty at 0.5 per cent is payable on all share purchases.

It will cost around £25.00 to buy or sell even a small amount of stock through a broker, but there are several cheap dealing services costing less. For details about these, watch the daily paper or write to the Stock Exchange (address on page 117).

The normal way for companies to raise money is through ordinary shares (as the name implies), and these are best for new investors. In addition, there are unsecured loan stocks, debentures, convertibles and preference shares. Some provide a fixed income or less risk, while others have features that are attractive only under certain circumstances. Dividends from stocks are usually paid with basic rate tax already deducted.

■ Note that it is possible to make up to £5,500 gains or profits from buying or selling stocks and shares before Capital Gains Tax has to be paid. A husband and wife each have this limit.

RULES FOR INVESTING

It is probably best to get professional advice, for there is always a risk involved when putting money on the stock market. But if you want to make your own investments, here are some simple rules:

- read the financial press and follow the radio and television programmes listed on page 119;
- spread your money among fixed interest stocks, unit trusts investing in overseas markets, and UK companies with a long record of growth;
- if you can afford a loss, invest in a 'speculative' share or two;
- avoid investing in too many companies, because of the monitoring and paperwork required;
- investments, including unit and investment trusts, may not show any gain for two years or more. Unless you have faith in your choice or can afford to wait for a 'turn-around', cut any losses early.

Privatised industries

Many people have bought shares in the privatised industries such as British Telecom and the water boards. If various members of your family applied separately for shares, and you now want to cut the cost of selling them, you could ask the registrar listed on the certificates to transfer all 'family shares' to one name. In doing this you may need a transfer certificate, and transferring shares could mean losing the right to a discount or bonus.

When buying or selling shares in the privatised industries, check on the dealing services for private investors, and be on the look-out for special discounts when advertised.

Investment trusts

One sound way to spread the risk associated with the stockmarket is to get into an investment trust. This is itself a quoted company issuing a fixed number of shares. The strength of a trust is that the capital is invested in various other companies, often spread among different countries. There are some 200 members of the Association of Investment Trust Companies (AITC) which provides a monthly information sheet (address on page 114).

Until recently, the only way to buy an investment trust was through a broker, but now most trusts have schemes for accepting lump sums or monthly savings. Often this is at a much lower commission, because the buying is done in bulk. Several investment trusts also reinvest the dividends for accumulated growth.

When you read that shares in an investment trust can be bought at a discount, this does not mean you can get a cheaper price than the one quoted in the newspapers. The discount refers to the amount by which the share price is cheaper than the net value of the assets held by the trust. The discount is an advantage where income is concerned because the dividend is likely to be bigger than the average dividend of the companies invested in. But this discount could mean some loss of capital if it is higher when you sell.

INDIRECT INVESTMENTS

Unit trusts

These remain a popular form of investment because there is a certain level of safety compared with investing directly in stocks and shares. For a start, the managers who run the fund on a daily basis are accountable to trustees (usually the big banks) which hold the assets by law.

In all cases, a unit trust puts together the sums invested by unit-holders and spreads the total among a number of stocks and shares. Although a trust will have holdings in many companies, it cannot put more than 10 per cent of the fund into any one of them.

There are two ways to buy unit trusts – either with a lump sum or by regular savings of at least £20.00. For an outright purchase, the minimum is around £250, but most trusts are geared to higher lump sums (£500 plus). There are also 'designated accounts' which can be opened by an adult such as a grandparent in the name of a minor and made over to the grandchild on attaining 18 years. Only the adult can withdraw the money before then.

Unit prices as well as the fund's charges are published daily in newspapers or magazines. Three prices are given: the lower or 'bid' price is the one at which you sell back the units to the management company; the higher or 'offer' is the price at which you buy them. There is also a 'cancellation' price, the minimum price at which the trust will buy back your shares. When there are many sellers the cancellation price could be lower than the normal bid price.

Between bid and offer prices there is a gap of about 6 per cent, which means that each unit-holder pays an initial charge of around 5 to 6 per cent. There is also an annual management fee of about 1 per cent, as explained in the unit's prospectus and annual report.

The value of the units must, therefore, rise by at least 6 per cent before there is any gain for you on selling. But trusts must always be thought of as medium- to long-term investments to be held for at least three years. There should also be a return from the dividends or interest on the shares or stocks which the unit trust holds. These 'distributions' may be made monthly, quarterly, biannually or yearly. In an 'accumulation' unit, the distributions go back into your holding.

■ Note that the prospectus of any authorised unit trust must state that the price of units can go down as well as up.

PROTECTION FOR UNIT-HOLDERS

Unit trusts can be bought through newspaper advertisements or through insurance companies and a wide range of intermediaries such as building societies, banks and stockbrokers. Any commission is already included in the management company's initial charge, but discounts may be available. As of March 1991, Woolwich Building Society was buying and selling unit trusts over the counter; but there may be others also offering this by the summer.

You should buy unit trusts only from a member of one of the self-regulatory organisations such as the Financial Intermediaries, Managers & Brokers Association (FIMBRA) or a Recognised Professional Body (accountants, solicitors, etc).

In the event of a complaint, grievance or dissatisfaction, you should first contact the management of the unit trust company, giving as much information as possible, including the unit certificate number when available. If you are not satisfied with the response received, the management company must by law refer you to the appropriate Self-Regulatory Organisation: either the Life Assurance & Unit Trust Regulatory Organisation (LAUTRO) or the Investment Management Regulatory Organisation (IMRO) whose addresses are on pages 115–116.

DIFFERENT TYPES OF UNIT TRUSTS

Over 1,300 different trusts are available to the investing public, from 180 unit trust management groups. They can be classed as follows:

- Those aiming for capital growth, often achieved by buying good company shares and ploughing back all dividends and interest into the trust.

- Those intended for income either from fixed interest securities or from companies with a good record for rising dividends, so that the unit-holder can expect a slowly rising income rather than quick gains.

- There are also 'balanced' trusts, which try for a mixture of income and growth; and cash funds which invest mainly in the money markets.

- Specialised trusts invest in specific sectors such as smaller companies, fixed interest, gilts or in specific areas such as Europe or Japan, or a 'mix' of overseas markets. Specialised unit trusts tend to be more volatile than the broadly based general ones.

FACTORS TO CONSIDER

For a first investor, it is probably wiser to go for a UK general trust; and, if you are liable to the higher rate of tax, a growth one. However, the older you are, the more likely you are to prefer an income trust.

When markets are unstable, a 'pure' cash unit trust can prove useful as a higher return, lower risk investment. Cash funds are offered by Fidelity, Gartmore, Mercury, MIM Britannia, Save & Prosper and similar groups listed in the *Financial Times, Daily Telegraph* and other newspapers under the heading Authorised Unit Trusts.

In the rarer 'majority' cash unit trusts, such as those offered by Barings, Hambros and Stewart Ivory, 10 per cent or more of the funds are held in assets, normally in foreign currencies, which are indexed for Capital Gains Tax purposes. Because of their nature, there is virtually no fluctuation; and a loss approximating to the rate of inflation annually can be used to offset chargeable gains taken on other investments.

Regular purchases of unit trusts even out the ebb and flow of prices. This 'cost price averaging' avoids the problem of only buying units when the demand is great, and prices are correspondingly high.

The size of a fund should never be equated to risk. Some newer companies like Allied Dunbar and Standard Life now rival in size the older ones such as M & G (1931) and Save And Prosper. The nature of the investments (as detailed in the trust's deed) rather than size determines risk.

■ But whatever unit trust you choose, remember that this is not a short-term investment, and there is no guarantee of the return you seek.

For more information, read the leaflet *What Unit Trusts are all About*, available from the Unit Trust Association at the address on page 118.

Personal Equity Plans

This kind of fund is offered by banks, unit trust groups, investment trust houses, stockbrokers, insurance companies and building societies to enable small investors to participate in Britain's free enterprise.

A personal equity plan (PEP) may be bought by anybody over the age of 18, provided your application form contains your National Insurance or Pension Number. The dividends earned are free of income tax, and any profit you make from cashing in is not subject to Capital Gains Tax. You can invest in one PEP during each tax year up to a maximum of £6,000. Half of this may go into a unit or investment trust. A further £3,000 may also be invested in a one-company PEP. Alternatively, you can opt for a fund entirely composed of unit or investment trusts, with the maximum then being £3,000. For more details, see the free leaflet published by the Stock Exchange and the PEP guide listed on page 119.

In assessing PEPs, the following factors are worth considering if you are a taxpayer.

- Firstly, the time lag: PEPs must be regarded as very long-term investments like a pension plan, a life assurance policy or a mortgage. Short-term PEP investors are most unlikely ever to make enough profit from a PEP to reach the Capital Gains Tax threshold of £5,500.
- Secondly, the cost of investing in a PEP varies widely and may wipe out any possible early gains. Before investing, make sure you know what the plan's management charges are.
- Finally, there is the advantage of flexibility, with withdrawals, whenever made, being free of tax. You can use PEPs to boost up a pension; you can get your hands on the cash at any time, though different schemes have different rules about withdrawals. If you retire overseas, you can still draw your PEP income, though you cannot add to the capital. When you die,there will be something left for your heirs.

Income and Growth bonds

These are offered by insurance companies. You give up a lump sum over an agreed period, ranging from one to five years in return for a yearly fixed income (income bond) and the return of your capital at the end of the period.

When the interest is rolled up and paid back with your original investment, it is known as a growth bond. The minimum investment is £1,000, but there is no maximum. There may be a penalty for cashing in early.

FACTORS TO CONSIDER

- These bonds are quite good for standard rate taxpayers, as the fixed interest is paid net and guaranteed. Higher rate taxpayers might be liable to Income Tax and should not invest in a growth bond until there is an expectation of their income falling, for example, on retirement. Age Allowance too could be affected by income from the bonds.

- Interest rates on the money market could rise above that fixed for your bond, so think hard before committing your lump sum for several years, and invest only in a reputable company registered in Britain.

CREATING AN INVESTMENT PORTFOLIO

A portfolio must take into account your circumstances as an investor. With a lump sum, you should consider safety, amount, tax and time. A good general rule is always to spread the risk by holding different kinds of investments, including unit and investment trusts. These put your money with that of others into a pooled fund to buy a wide range of investments. But do remember that even such 'pooled' investments can go down as well as up.

As an example, *The Sunday Times Survey of Unit Trust Managers for 1990* showed that not a single unit trust investing in equities (ordinary shares) gained money for its investors during that year. The only equity invested unit trust that made a profit in 1990 was Exeter High Income Fund, specialising in income shares of split capital investment trusts. Otherwise only gilt and fixed interest funds (excluded from the survey) did well. However, another year, the best returns could come from equities or equity based funds.

But equities always carry risk. High taxpayers prepared to take risks to achieve tax advantages or capital growth can look at more sophisticated investments. Among them are the following:

- Warrants which offer the chance of buying shares in the future at an agreed price today.
- Traded options which allow an investor for an agreed price to buy and sell stock options without purchasing the actual shares.
- Business Expansion Schemes which give tax relief on investments of up to £40,000 per year in venture capital schemes if held for five years when, hopefully, capital plus growth comes back.

■ Note that these investments are not suitable for non-taxpayers, and only rarely for individuals paying basic-rate tax.

If you have a small amount of capital (by Stock Exchange standards) such as £10,000 or below, this should be invested mainly in building society accounts, National Savings or interest bearing bank deposits. A portion might also go into a TESSA or for the longer term (as long as the charges do not outweigh the tax benefits) a PEP.

Unit trusts are also longer term investments, so money that might be needed in an emergency should not be put into them. If you want to invest a small lump sum, say £5,000, in unit trusts, about half the amount could go into an income oriented fund and the remainder might be split between a growth and a general international fund. The division and choice depend on the investor's needs.

To illustrate how you create a portfolio with the greater flexibility of £50,000 to invest, the examples on the following pages show how a single person or a couple could aim to increase their income and protect it against inflation.

Example of a single person

Peggy Smith, a widow aged 62, is a basic-rate taxpayer with 3 adult children, and 4 grandchildren. Her savings and the proceeds from a life assurance on her husband's life total £50,000. This is currently in a building society, producing £4,500 a year. She receives a State Pension and works part-time at a salary of £4,160. Her home, worth £75,000, has no mortgage.

Aim: Peggy wants to make small gifts to her children, grandchildren and to charity, while at the same time protecting her capital against inflation and retaining flexibility. She reduces the amount in her building society account but safeguards her remaining income and capital with guaranteed income bonds and high coupon gilts bought at or below par. A personal pension contribution provides her with an extra pension, albeit small, which she can take out at any time before she reaches the age of 75 years.

Peggy's portfolio might look like this

	Amount invested/ given £	Annual income after tax £
Building society account	15,600	1,560.00
Income bond (guaranteed for 4 years)	6,000	591.00
TESSA (withdrawing net income)	3,000	300.00
Gilt (near par value, short dated, high coupon)	3,000	278.00
Gilt (5-year, under par value)	3,000	209.00
Unit trusts (growth oriented)	8,000	400.00
National Savings certificates	5,000	475.00
Investment trust (split capital, income shares)	2,900	230.00
Pension contribution	1,000	00.00
Gifts (4 x £250 + 3 x £300)	1,900	00.00
Gift to charity	600	00.00
	50,000	4,043.00

Example of a married couple

Eric Brown, made redundant at age 58, has savings and a redundancy lump sum of £25,000. His wife Jane is 56 and still working, and her salary covers the loan interest on their mortgage. They have no children at home.

Aim: The Browns want to keep their head above water until Eric gets another job, or their pensions become due. He has two options: to organise his own savings or use one of the few firms who will manage a 'small' sum of £25,000. If Eric decides to manage his portfolio himself, he should aim for the highest income and return of capital at the end of seven years when he will get the State and a (small) company pension.

The Browns' portfolio might look like this

	Amount invested £	Annual Income after tax £
Building society account (highest interest possible)	15,000	1,500
TESSA (withdrawing net interest)	3,000	300
Income bond (guaranteed for 5 years)	5,000	475
Unit trusts (split investment)	2,000	120
	25,000	2,395

After five years the Browns can review the situation with regard to the spread of the investment.

SUMMARY

Even when you have a lump sum of much less than £50,000 to invest, you should still split up the capital, with the equity element being smaller.

A portfolio should be monitored from time to time, and if you do not wish, or feel unable, to do this, you could use a stockbroker or investment manager. The charge would be about 1 per cent per year on the value of the portfolio, plus commission on individual transactions.

A word in private.

Capel-Cure Myers offers private investors a wide range of investment services. Whichever one suits your needs, you will have the peace of mind which comes from knowing that your investment affairs are being looked after by people with many years experience of even the most difficult markets. (We can trace our origins back nearly 200 years).

We can offer independent advice on all financial matters including personal portfolio management, stocks and shares, Personal Equity Plans, unit trusts and bonds. In addition, our independent financial services subsidiary provides a range of financial planning services including annuities and Inheritance Tax planning.

If you would like a private word, please contact John Kennett on 071 488 0707 or write to him at The Registry, Royal Mint Court, London EC3N 4EY.

CAPEL-CURE MYERS
CAPITAL MANAGEMENT

Dedicated to the management of money

CAPEL-CURE MYERS CAPITAL MANAGEMENT LIMITED.
MEMBER OF THE SECURITIES AND FUTURES AUTHORITY
AND THE LONDON STOCK EXCHANGE.
REGISTERED OFFICE: THE REGISTRY, ROYAL MINT COURT, LONDON EC3N 4EY.

FORGET ABOUT FUNERAL COSTS!

- Chosen Heritage provides a guaranteed funeral when required, at *today's* price, at any point in the future.
- Chosen Heritage spares trouble and expense for your family.
- Chosen Heritage gives you peace of mind, knowing that all the arrangements are made and paid for.

Thousands of people have joined the Chosen Heritage scheme so they can forget about funeral costs. These are not insurance policies but a practical way to make arrangements in advance.

Simply return this coupon for your free brochure or call now on **FREEPHONE 0800 525 555**.

Completely confidential. No salesman will call.

RECOMMENDED BY

AGE *Concern*

selected 'Best Buy' in recent survey

CHOSEN HERITAGE LIMITED FREEPOST, EAST GRINSTEAD, RH19 1ZA

CUSTODIAN TRUSTEE: BARCLAYS BANK PLC

Please send me your brochure, with no obligation.

Name: _____

Address: _____

_____

_____ Post Code: _____ AC

Other Financial Options

This part of the book presents an overview of occupational and personal pensions with the names of organisations which can help with queries and further information. In addition, for people approaching retirement, there is a summary of various life assurance options; and for elderly retired people, a review of annuities.

Home-owners interested in using the value of their property as a source of capital will find details about home income and reversion schemes and information about insuring their property and its contents as well as a car.

For people thinking ahead about disposing of their assets, there is guidance about making a Will and investing in a funeral plan.

PENSION PLANNING

The most important rule about pensions is to plan early. Retirement always comes sooner than you think. When approaching this leisure age, work out exactly what you can expect from the various State, occupational and/or private schemes. There is also the fact that you receive tax relief on all pension contributions. This section gives an overview of the pensions now available.

State and occupational pensions

The first tier of the State scheme is the Basic Pension, paid for by National Insurance contributions, as explained in detail in Age Concern's publication *Your Rights* (see page 122 for how to order).

The second tier is the State Earnings Related Pension Scheme (SERPS) which provides earnings related benefits in addition to the Basic Pension for people who are not part of a 'contracted out' occupational (employer's) scheme. Very approximately, the maximum benefit from twenty years within SERPS could double the amount received from the Basic Pension (depending on your working life, earnings, etc). For people retiring after the year 2000 the Government is reducing the amount you will receive from SERPS, so for anyone aged 40 or less, it may be beneficial to consider leaving or contracting out of SERPS and investing instead in a personal pension.

Prior to 1 July 1988 an employer could make it a condition of employment to join the company (occupational) scheme. Since that date employees have had the option to join or not. Opting out may be desirable for someone without job security or intending to change jobs often throughout their career. However, most of the big occupational schemes have upgraded their benefits and these may seem more attractive than a personal pension.

To improve the amount of pension payable on retirement, employees may also pay additional voluntary contributions (AVCs) into their occupational scheme or a 'free standing' scheme (FSAVC) – provided their total contributions do not exceed 15 per cent of earnings.

Limited price indexing of occupational pensions will be introduced in the near future so that part of a pension will increase in line with prices, up to 5 per cent a year. Restrictions are also being placed on how companies use any surplus cash in their pension funds, requiring that they introduce indexing for members of their schemes who are still working, as well as for retired members and early leavers. Good company schemes already have indexed rates.

Until recently the majority of occupational schemes have had different retirement ages, usually in line with those for the State Pension. This sexual discrimination has been called into question by a European Court judgement which states that discrimination is illegal. At the moment the outcome of this ruling is unclear, and it may be another year before the matter is clarified. (Note that the judgement does not directly affect the unequal retirement ages for the State pensions.) Therefore we recommend that you seek professional advice if you are either moving jobs or retiring early.

Personal pensions

Before retiring, someone without a company pension should invest as soon as possible in a personal pension. People already in one should note that the Government has recently changed the rules about them so that on the whole, starting a new pension is more attractive than ever.

Since July 1988, Self-Employed Pension Contracts, otherwise known as Section 226 policies, have ceased to be available for purchase; but if you were already paying annual premiums into a Section 226 policy before that date, you can continue to do so. From the age of 60 you can draw up to 30 per cent of the fund as a lump sum. The balance left in the fund purchases an annuity paying an income for the rest of your life.

Since 1 July 1988 only personal pensions have been available. These allow you to take 25 per cent of the fund as a lump sum on retirement. The schemes also allow you to retire from age 50. The contributions maximum for personal pensions is more generous than that for Section 226 policies, but for both kinds of pensions you can continue paying contributions until the age of 75. Both employees and employers as well as self-employed people can contribute to the new style arrangements.

The choice between the various personal pensions is complicated, so get independent advice from more than one source before committing yourself, and do check the latest regulations. If you have dependants and do not have adequate life assurance, do not allow the policy to be worded so that only the instalments are returned if you die before drawing the pension. Make sure the fund's full value is to be returned.

Consumer protection

The Social Security Act 1990 introduced new consumer protection measures which affect pensioners. Both occupational and personal pension schemes must register with a central body by 31 July 1991, and the Occupational Pensions Board has been appointed as Registrar (address on page 116). Its main purpose is to establish a tracing service to help individuals who have lost touch with their former employers to track down their pension rights.

Since April 1991, a Pensions Ombudsman has been dealing with complaints about company and personal pensions. However, the Occupational Pensions Advisory Service still acts as the first port of call for information and advice (address on page 116). The Inland Revenue also has departments which deal with queries about pensions (address on page 115).

LIFE ASSURANCE AND ANNUITIES

Life assurance

Before investing in a life policy, you should question whether you really need to protect your dependants against your death, and if so, for how long and for how much? If you are a member of an occupational pension scheme, and you should die prematurely, will it provide enough income for your dependants?

Life assurance can be divided into four types: whole of life; term or temporary assurance; endowment; and annuity.

A whole life policy pays out on death whenever that occurs, but is often unnecessary and expensive. For anybody over 50, it should only be considered when there is a potentially serious Inheritance Tax liability, and all other steps to minimise that liability have been taken.

Term assurance is basic and cheap; the cost will rise the older you are when you take out cover. You pay premiums for a limited period, but only if you die within the term does the company pay. The latest variant being offered by the insurance world is a scheme which provides compensation in the event of terminal illness. However, for anyone over 65 'dread disease' cover is likely to be very expensive and probably inappropriate.

Endowment assurance is a method of saving for a guaranteed payment at the end of a fixed number of years or your earlier death. Unlike term assurance, money always comes back either to you or, if you die within the term, to your heirs. Because endowment assurance is more expensive, someone with this kind of cover may be tempted to surrender a policy to meet the expense of certain emergency situations. It is often not beneficial to surrender an endowment policy, especially if you are getting tax relief on one started before 14 March 1984.

Where it is appropriate to surrender an endowment policy, it may be worth exploring the possibility of selling at auction.

You should use one of the firms who specialise in auctioning insurance policies, as they can usually get a higher price than would be the case if the policy were surrendered to the insurance company.

If you do decide to surrender an endowment policy, you should get professional advice about the tax implications. Then get a quote from the insurance company and compare it with what you are offered by one of the auctioning firms. They include Foster and Cranfield (address on page 115) who have been running monthly auctions of insurance policies for many years, usually held at the New Connaught Rooms in London. Another firm is Policy Network (071–938 3626) which prefers endowments with under fifteen years to run, from good quality companies, and aims to sell a policy within a month.

On the other hand, if you wish to invest in a second-hand endowment policy on someone else's life, note that their early death will limit its value. At all events, you may be liable to Capital Gains Tax; and there could be other tax complications.

Annuities

Annuities are the reverse of other kinds of life assurance. You put up a lump sum to get income either for a fixed period or for the remainder of your lifetime. The older you are, the higher your income will be. If you are 70 or over and have no heirs and come from a long-lived family, a lifetime annuity can offer attractions.

Annuities are sold by insurance companies in a variety of forms: one where payment is guaranteed for five or ten years, even if you die within that period; a joint annuity for husband and wife where the income is paid until the death of the last survivor; or one with a 5 per cent escalating rate to (partly) offset inflation.

The minimum sum required to buy an annuity is around £1,000. The income may be paid in arrears or in advance, half yearly or annually. How much you get from each £1,000 of capital invested depends on the insurance company chosen, the conditions of the annuity and interest rates at the time of purchase.

FACTORS TO CONSIDER

Unless the annuity offers an escalating rate, the income you receive will remain fixed from the outset, so you gain most if you buy when interest rates are high and likely to fall.

Part of a purchased annuity is regarded as repayment of capital, and this amount is free of Income Tax. A compulsory annuity, paid as a pension on retirement, does not have this concession, but is added to your overall income. If your income is sufficiently low to make you a non-taxpayer, you can arrange with the company to receive income gross.

An annuity which pays an income for a short fixed term can be useful to bridge the gap before an improvement in your circumstances. For example, if you are made redundant at 60 but your pension is paid from the age of 65, your redundancy payment could provide an annuity income in the meantime. However, before investing in an annuity, you should get independent advice and consider other investment possibilities.

RAISING CAPITAL FROM YOUR HOME

Home-owners interested in cashing in on the value of their home may want to invest in a home income plan (sometimes called a mortgage annuity) or a home reversion scheme. However, before entering into an agreement for one of these options which uses the value of your property, you should consider very carefully all the factors involved – such as the effect on any State benefits you receive and what would happen if you should subsequently want to move. As with all investments, you should get independent legal and financial advice.

Home income plans

With these, the money from a loan, secured against the value of your property, is used to buy an annuity which provides a guaranteed monthly income for life. Part of this is used to pay off the loan interest, and the rest is yours to spend as you wish. In deciding whether to opt for one of these plans, you should consider the following points.

- Age is an essential factor – the older you are, the bigger the annuity income. You must be at least 70, or, for a couple, have a combined age of 150 years. If you should die soon after taking out a plan, your heirs will have to pay off the original loan from the estate, and you will not have received much income. There is a 'capital protected' home income plan designed to cover this situation, but at a price.

- Whether the loan interest is fixed or variable is another factor. For plans offering a variable interest rate, note that if the rate increases, your income will decrease. Schemes with a fixed interest rate are much more reliable.

- Inflation can also reduce the value of home income plans, as they are not index-linked.

- Because tax relief is only available on £30,000 of mortgage repayments, this limits the size of loan you can get.

Home reversion schemes

When you invest in one of these schemes, you actually sell your home to a reversion company for a lump sum or an annuity income while you continue to live in it. On your death or on the death of both partners in the case of a married couple, the property passes to the reversion company. Some schemes have special features, such as one where the annuity income is index-linked to the value of all the properties in the scheme, which are valued every two years.

Letting your home

An alternative way of raising money from your home is of course by letting it (perhaps while you are on a long-stay holiday abroad), or by having a lodger. The tax implications are covered in more detail on page 41.

The Factsheet listed on page 119 gives more detailed information about home income plans and other ways of raising money from your home. There is also the Age Concern book *Using Your Home as Capital* (details on page 121).

GENERAL INSURANCE COVER

There are several kinds of general insurance which you may already have or may be considering such as insuring the structure of your house and its contents, as well as your clothing and possessions when you travel, your car and possibly a boat. You can also insure your health, with tax relief available on premiums for policies taken out for someone over the age of 60 as outlined on page 23.

Property and household contents

When considering the various policies, note that the cost can vary considerably between different providers. This applies particularly to buildings insurance, where you may well be able to find better rates with an insurance company or broker compared with the premiums charged by your building society or other mortgage provider.

Special rates for retired people are available from a number of different organisations, including the household buildings and contents scheme provided by Age Concern Insurance Services (address on page 114). Some insurers also give discounts to policy holders who install smoke alarms and additional security systems in their homes or live in an area with a Neighbourhood Watch Scheme. These discounts are particularly relevant in urban areas where there is a high risk of burglaries, and where some of the security requirements will be compulsory.

Some insurers are now developing policies based on the number of main rooms or bedrooms in your home. These policies do not have an exact sum insured related to the value of your contents, but usually carry an overall limit which is, generally speaking, higher than the actual amount at risk. These contracts are very simple and straight forward; but you should ensure that you are not paying too much for cover which you do not need and should compare the rates offered by several companies. In every case check the policy wording carefully and make sure that any articles of value are covered to the extent you require.

Travel insurance

Unless your household contents insurance makes special provision, it is unlikely that it will be an adequate substitute for travel insurance to cover clothing and personal possessions when you are abroad or away from home. Travel insurance policies carry certain restrictions, depending on your age, which can void certain sections of the policy. This is particularly relevant to medical insurance, and you should check your policy wording carefully or discuss it with the company concerned before you travel.

Motor insurance

This is another area where many retired people are likely to be offered better premium rates, but you should still look very carefully at the cover provided to ensure that it is adequate. If you are over the age of 70, many insurance policies will have certain restrictions, and you may be required to have a medical examination when the contract is due for renewal. This could also apply if you are involved in an accident, so it is worth checking these details especially if you are contemplating changing your insurance.

Age Concern Insurance Services provide a special motor insurance policy, which has been specially designed to provide motorists aged 60 and over with wide ranging cover at competitive rates. However, it is also worth checking the rates of a number of other organisations which specialise in motor insurance for older people. The rates will usually be cheapest where driving is restricted to the owner only or to the husband and wife; and as with household insurance, rates will vary according to the area where you live.

FUNERAL PLANNING AND MAKING A WILL

'In this world, nothing is certain but death and taxes', wrote Benjamin Franklin. So there is nothing morbid in thinking ahead about burial. Thrift clubs for funerals are well established in Britain. It is advisable to make provisional plans for both your own and any partner's funeral so as to avoid expense and anxiety for all concerned when death occurs. Also useful are some written instructions, either in or with your Will, about whether you wish to be buried or cremated and where you wish this to take place.

Obviously you should try to ensure that enough money will be readily available to cover the likely cost of the funeral. The Odd Fellows (Manchester) survey gave the average cost of funerals in 1990 as basic £638 plus disbursements of £282; cremations £533 (basic) plus disbursements of £179. Dying away from home is even more expensive.

If you are actually arranging a funeral, you should get a written estimate of the cost at least a day before. Also note that there are widespread regional variations in the current prices. Moreover, there is concern that some undertakers may not be abiding by the code of practice laid down by the National Association of Funeral Directors (address on page 116).

The association offers two plans for pre-payment for funerals, provides a simple service for a basic funeral and operates a conciliation service for complaints against its members. Chosen Heritage (address on page 115) in association with Age Concern England also offers pre-payment plans, as do the friendly societies and a few insurance companies.

For those without enough means to pay for a simple funeral, there is a Funeral Payment available from the Social Fund, provided that the deceased person did not leave enough money to cover the expenses or that the person responsible for the funeral is entitled to Income Support, Housing Benefit or Community Charge Benefit. To get help from the Social Fund, ask at the social security office for a form SF 200.

The Age Concern publication *Your Rights* (see page 121 for price) has complete details of the Social Fund.

Making a Will

It is most important to make a Will so that your assets are disposed of as you wish, that dependants are provided for and heirs do not pay tax unnecessarily. In Scotland, 75 per cent of people wait until they are over 60 before making a Will, and in Britain two out of every three people never make a Will at all.

Solicitors earn a lot of money out of 'decoding' badly worded documents, so it's worth taking care with your written instructions. A Will must be signed and witnessed by two people who do not stand to inherit from it. In Scotland, where the law is different, if the Will is in your own handwriting (a holograph, as it is called), you do not need to have your signature witnessed, and there are certain prior rights which can be claimed by relatives.

Unknown or missing Wills can cause a lot of trouble, so make sure you have only one, preferably lodged in a bank or with a solicitor and that all concerned know where to find it. Under the Courts and Legal Services Act of 1990, a Will can now be prepared by financial institutions such as banks, building societies and insurance companies as well as by solicitors.

If you die intestate (without a Will), the money and goods which you have left are divided among members of your family according to rules laid down by law; or if there is no near kin, what you have left goes to the State. Your partner is automatically entitled to money in a joint bank or post office savings account and to joint named National Savings Certificates - except for those nominated before May 1981 to be paid to someone else.

You can draw up a simple Will by yourself, or use a Will writing service; and there are leaflets and a book available to help, as listed on page 119.

Further Information

This part of Your Taxes and Savings *gives details about national organisations as a source of help and further information. In addition there is a list of publications and Age Concern England factsheets as well as radio and television programmes covering money matters. Also included is an Index to help you find the information you require in this book.*

USEFUL ADDRESSES

Age Concern Insurance Services
For special home insurance protection for buildings and contents. Also offers motor insurance.

Orbital House 85–87
Croydon Road
Caterham
Surrey CR3 5YZ
0883 346964

• **Association of Investment Trust Companies**
For information and list of investment trusts.

16 Finsbury Circus
London EC2M 7JJ
071–588 5347

Banking Ombudsman
For complaints against almost all popular banks – with arbitration.

5 Fetter Lane
London EC4 1BR
071-583 1395

BIIBA
Trade association for insurance and investment brokers.

14 Bevis Marks
London EC3A 7NT
071–623 9043

Building Societies Association
The trade association for all building societies.

3 Saville Row
London W1X 1AF
071–437 0655

Building Societies Ombudsman
Investigates most types of complaints, as listed in a pamphlet.

35–37 Grosvenor Gdns
London SW1X 7AW
071–931 0044

• **Building Society Shop**
Recommends the best buys in building society accounts.

City House
Maid Marian Way
Nottingham NG1 6BH
0602 472595

Capital Taxes Office
For current information about Inheritance Tax.

England and Wales	**Scotland**	**Northern Ireland**
Minford House	16 Picardy Place	Law Courts Building
Rockley Road	Edinburgh	Chichester Street
London W14 0DF	EH1 3NB	Belfast BT1 3NU

Chosen Heritage Ltd
Offers pre-arranged funeral payment schemes and a range of relevant information.

Farringdon House
East Grinstead
West Sussex
RH19 1EW
0342 312266

Corporate Estate Agents Ombudsman
For complaints about some estate agents.

PO Box 1014
Salisbury
Hants SP1 1YQ
0722 333 306

Council of Mortgage Lenders
Association representing mortgage lenders.

3 Saville Row
London W1X 1AF
071–437 0655

Department of National Savings
For general enquiries, especially by professional advisers.

375 Kensington
High Street
London W14 8SD
071–605 9300

FIMBRA
Self-regulatory organisation for financial intermediaries, managers, brokers.

Hertsmere House
Hertsmere Road
London E14 4AB
071–538 8860

Foster, E.H. and Cranfield
Auctioneers for life assurance endowment policies.

20 Britton Street
London EC1M 5NQ
071–608 1941

IMRO
For complaints about investment management.

Broadwalk House
5 Appold Street
London EC2A 2LL
071–628 6022

Inland Revenue
For enquiries about pensions.

Lynwood Road
Thames Ditton
Surrey KT7 0DP
081–398 4242

Insurance Ombudsman Bureau
For complaints about most insurance companies.

31 Southampton Row
London WC1B 5HJ
071–242 8613

Law Society
For complaints about its members who recommend investments.

52 Chancery Lane
London W2A 1SX
071–242 1222

LAUTRO
Self-regulatory organisation for assurance and unit trust sales.

103 New Oxford Street
London WC1A 1QH
071–379 0444

Legal Services Ombudsman
For complaints about barristers, solicitors and licensed conveyancers.

22 Oxford Court
Oxford Street
Manchester M2 3WQ
061–236 9532

Money Management Council
An educational resource centre for factsheets on money matters. Does not offer individual advice.

18 Doughty Street
London WC1N 2PL

National Association of Funeral Directors
Offers code of conduct and procedure.

618 Warwick Road
Solihull B91 1AA
021–711 1343

* National Savings
For Government stocks, income bonds.

Bonds and Stocks
Office
Blackpool FY3 9YP

For certificates, yearly plans, SAYE.

Millburngate House
Durham DH99 1NS
091–386 4900

For ordinary and investment accounts; capital bonds.

Glasgow G58 1SB
041–649 4565
041–636 2627

Occupational Pensions Advisory Service
For questions and complaints about occupational pensions.

11 Belgrave Road
London SW1V 1RB
071–233 8080

Occupational Pensions Board
For enquiries about 'contracted out' occupational pension schemes.

PO Box 2EE
Newcastle Upon Tyne
NE99 2EE

Occupational Pensions Ombudsman
*Works in association with
Occupational Pensions Advisory
Service.*

11 Belgrave Road
London SW1V 1RB
071–834 9144

Occupational Pensions Registry
*Newly formed information service
for tracing pensions.*

PO Box 1NN
Newcastle Upon Tyne
NE99 1NN

Office of Fair Trading
*Examines services to consumers,
publishes leaflets.*

Breams Buildings
London EC4A 1PR
071–242 2858

Office of Investment Referee
*For appeals for compensation from
an organisation which belongs to
IMRO.*

6 Frederick Place
London EC2R 8BT
071-796 3065

Registrar of Friendly Societies
*The trade association for friendly
societies.*

15 Great Marlborough
Street
London W1B 2AY
071–437 9992

**Securities and Futures Authority Ltd
(SFA)**
*Self-regulatory organisation for
stock and futures brokers and
advisers.*

Old Broad Street
London EC2N 1EQ
071–256 9000

Securities and Investments Board
*The authority to approach for
redress of grievances and for
information.*

3 Royal Exchange
Buildings
London EC3V 3NL
071–929 3652

Solicitors Complaints Bureau
*For compensation resulting from
inadequate service by a solicitor.*

Portland House
Stage Place
London SW1E 5BL
071 834 2288

Stock Exchange
*For free booklets and a list of
brokers for small investors.*

Throgmorton Street
London EC1N 1HP
071–588 2355

Unit Trust Association   65 Kingsway
For introductory booklet,   London WC2B 6TD
newsletter, enquiry guide, video.   071–831 0898

Unit Trust Ombudsman   31 Southampton Row
For complaints about unit trusts   London WC1B 5HJ
and some insurance companies.   071–242 8613

---

* National Savings current rates are available from one of the following numbers at any time:

personal calls: 071–605 9461

answerphone: 0253 723714, 041–632 2766, 071–605 9483

Barclays Bank free service for enquiries and complaints: 0800–282 390

PUBLICATIONS AND PROGRAMMES

FACTSHEETS FROM AGE CONCERN ENGLAND

Age Concern England produces a range of factsheets in addition to the ones listed below. Single copies available free on receipt of 9" x 6" sae to the address on page 120.

Raising an Income from Your Home Factsheet No 12
Community Charge and Older People Factsheet No 21
Making a Will Factsheet No 7
Arranging a Funeral Factsheet No 27
Instructions for My Next of Kin 25p; discount for bulk orders

OTHER PUBLICATIONS

Good Tessa Guide £12.00 published by Money Guides, Bury St Edmunds, Suffolk 1P 30 OSF, Tel: 0449 736287

Making a Will (free), *Making a Will Won't Kill You* 60p published by the Law Society, Tel: 071–242 1222

Wills and Probate (1990) £7.95 published by the Consumers' Association, Tel: 071–486 5544

PEP Guide (1990) £8.95 published by Chase de Vere Investments PLC, Tel: 071–404 5766

MAGAZINES AND NEWSPAPERS

Building Society Choice. Useful for investors. Published by Money Guides, Tel:0449 736287.

Daily Telegraph. For prices of stocks, shares and unit trusts.

Financial Times. Stock exchange and other market prices.

Planned Savings. For insurance and investments.

Money Management. For unit trusts and pensions.

Pensions World. Articles mainly on occupational pensions.

RADIO AND TELEVISION PROGRAMMES

Money Box BBC Radio 4 on Saturday and Monday mornings.
The Money Programme BBC2 on Sunday evenings.
Channel 4 Daily 6.20 am onwards.

ABOUT AGE CONCERN

Your Taxes and Savings is one of a wide range of publications produced by Age Concern England – National Council on Ageing. In addition, Age Concern is actively engaged in training, information provision, research and campaigning for retired people and those who work with them. It is a registered charity dependent on public support for the continuation of its work.

Age Concern England links closely with Age Concern centres in Scotland, Wales and Northern Ireland to form a network of over 1,400 independent local UK groups. These groups, with the invaluable help of an estimated 250,000 volunteers, aim to improve the quality of life for older people and develop services appropriate to local needs and resources. These include advice and information, day care, visiting services, transport schemes, clubs, and specialist facilities for physically and mentally frail older people.

Age Concern England
1268 London Road
London SW16 4ER
Tel: 081–679 8000

Age Concern Wales
4th Floor
1 Cathedral Road
Cardiff CF1 9SD
Tel: 0222 371821/371566

Age Concern Scotland
54a Fountainbridge
Edinburgh EH3 9PT
Tel: 031–228 5656

Age Concern Northern Ireland
6 Lower Crescent
Belfast BT7 1NR
Tel: 0232 245729

PUBLICATIONS FROM AGE CONCERN

A wide range of titles is published under the Age Concern imprint.

MONEY MATTERS

Your Rights 1991/92
Sally West
A highly acclaimed annual guide to the State Benefits available to older people. Contains current information on Income Support, Housing Benefit and Retirement Pensions, among other matters, and provides advice on how to claim.
£2.15   0–86242–105–5

Using Your Home as Capital
Cecil Hinton
This best selling book for home-owners, which is updated annually, gives a detailed explanation of how to capitalize on the value of your home and obtain regular additional income.
£3.50   0–86242-107-1

Managing Other People's Money
Penny Letts
The management of money and property is usually a personal and private matter. However, there may come a time when someone else has to take over on either a temporary or permanent basis. This book looks at the circumstances in which such a need could arise and provides a step-by-step guide to the arrangements which have to be made.
£5.95   0–86242–090–3

GENERAL

Living, Loving and Ageing: Sexual and personal relationships in later life
Wendy Greengross and Sally Greengross
Sexuality is often regarded as the preserve of the younger generation. At last, here is a book for older people and those

who work with them, which tackles the issues in a straightforward fashion, avoiding preconceptions and bias.
£4.95   0–86242–070–9

Taking Good Care: A handbook for care assistants
Jenyth Worsley
Examines all aspects of the caring process, whether the carer is an assistant in a Residential Home or looking after an elderly friend or relative at home.
£6.95   0–86242–072–5

Life in the Sun: A guide to long-stay holidays and living abroad in retirement
Nancy Tuft
For older people considering long-stay holidays or moving abroad. This essential guide examines topics varying from pets to poll tax.
£6.95   0–86242–085–7

HEALTH

Your Health in Retirement
Dr J A Muir Gray and Pat Blair
A comprehensive guide to help people look after their health. Full details are given of health advisers and useful organisations to contact for help.
£4.50   0–86242–082–2

To order books, send a cheque or money order to the address below. Credit card orders may be made on 081–679 8000.

Age Concern England (DEPT TS2)
FREEPOST
1268 London Road
London SW16 4ER

We hope you found this book useful. If so, perhaps you would like to receive further information about Age Concern or help us do more for elderly people.

Dear Age Concern
Please send me the details I've ticked below:

other publications
☐

Age Concern special offers
☐

volunteer with a local group
☐

regular giving
☐

covenant
☐

legacy
☐

Meantime, here is a gift of

£ _____ PO/CHEQUE or VISA/ACCESS No _____

NAME (BLOCK CAPITALS) _____

SIGNATURE _____

ADDRESS _____

_____

_____ POSTCODE _____

Please pull out this page and send it to: **Age Concern** (DEPT TS2)
FREEPOST
1268 London Road
no stamp needed **London SW16 4EJ**

INDEX